MAKING CHRISTIAN
DECISIONS

MAKING CHRISTIAN DECISIONS

by

George Newlands

Dean of Trinity Hall, Cambridge

MOWBRAY
LONDON & OXFORD

Copyright © George Newlands 1985

ISBN 0 264 66970 3

First published 1985
by A.R. Mowbray & Co. Ltd,
Saint Thomas House, Becket Street,
Oxford, OX1 1SJ

Typeset by Oxford Publishing Services, Oxford
Printed in Great Britain by Biddles Ltd, Guildford.

British Library Cataloguing in Publication Data

Newlands, George M.
    Making Christian decisions.—(Mowbrays Christian studies
    series)
    1. Christian ethics
    I. Title
    241   BJ1251

    ISBN 0–264–66970–3

In memoriam
G W H L

CONTENTS

Preface

God is love. God is in his essential nature self-giving love. This affirmation lies at the centre of the Christian gospel. What does the understanding of God as love mean for ethics, for human relationships, individual and social, in our world? The purpose of this book is to provide a short account of the implications of God's love for our response to a number of highly particular and urgent ethical issues in the modern world.

This is not an essay in the theoretical analysis of the concept of self-giving love, and it is not an essay in the long tradition of studies of Christianity and the world order. Though I hope that in the course of the argument light will be shed on these matters. I concentrate here on a selection of specific issues.

Considerable space is devoted to the problems of peace and war. This is, in many ways, in my view *the* problem, for it diverts immense resources away from the maintenance of civilized standards of care for most of the world's population. The second main theme centres on issues of personal relationships, sex and marriage, and legal and medical ethical issues. To take but one example, if the considerable intellectual and material labours devoted by Christians to opposition to birth control were diverted to the problem of peace, the planet might be saved from two gigantic interrelated and self-inflicted disasters. The last section considers the meaning of justice within the conflicting interests of society.

The theoretical questions raised by Christian ethics are not easy. But if faith has any connection with practice, it has to be possible to provide some straight answers to live by. No man or woman can or should decide for another. Much of the time we may not think about basic ethical issues. But when they come up in our lives, and decisions are required, we often benefit from the sharing of ideas and experience. Here then are some reflections, offered not as authoritative pronouncements but as considered suggestions. I am grateful to Keith Ward and to William Purcell for some valuable comments on the manuscript, and to my wife for encouraging me to write on ethics.

George Newlands
Trinity Hall, Cambridge, 1984

1. Making Moral Decisions

'A Christian lives in Christ through faith, and in his neighbour through love.' This is how Martin Luther summed up the Christian life. Through Jesus Christ comes faith in God, creator and reconciler, source of all being, the one whose loving concern sustains and supports the whole fabric of the universe. The life of faith constantly involves thinking for others, acting in concern for other people. Reflection upon such action involves Christian ethics. As individuals we are concerned with personal ethics in our relationships with other individuals. As persons in society and members of the Christian community we are concerned with social ethics, with relationships in society as a whole and in Christian responsibility towards all human beings. We seek answers to the question of how life is to be lived in faithful discipleship to Jesus Christ.

Countless books have been written on the principles of ethics. Ethics without reflection on methods and principles would clearly be a difficult enterprise. Christian ethics asks for the meaning of discipleship. It enquires into the nature and operation of love and it considers God's law, conscience, the practical situations in which ethical issues arise. It analyses the meaning of justice, of a loving and a caring society, and it scrutinizes the ethics of scholarly and scientific research. Beyond this, it goes back to the basic issues of creation and creativity, of forgiveness and reconciliation, the grace of God and the peace of God.[1]

What is a Christian decision and how is it arrived at? Decisions are not reached easily. In the history of the Christian community there have been many decisions. However, the quick decisions have not always been the right ones and the wise decisions have often been the result of painstaking and difficult deliberation. Today we live in a pluralist society in which different standards and values abound. Decisions, it often seems, are too difficult for us: we must leave them to the experts. But it would be strange indeed if faith had no bearing on the conduct of life, if grace were the subject only of singing hymns in church rather than the source of action.

In the Churches there are different approaches to decisions in the various denominations and theological traditions. We have to develop the capacity to decide between these different approaches. We need all the experience and observation of humanity that we can get. We may see the ultimate shape of humanity as God's humanity, and we understand human life to be dependent on and grounded in the life of God. Our basic parable of human action is the life and teaching of Jesus Christ, within the framework of the reconciling activity of God, creator and redeemer. We want to affirm that the love of God sustains all humanity, even where God is not experienced as a presence: therefore Christian ethics is always driven back from the source in God's love to the concrete particulars. In the course of exploration we shall want to seek guidance from biblical narrative, historical tradition, contemporary theology and ethics, cognate disciplines in the modern world. We must try to ensure that the core elements of an adequate understanding of ethics are present in every case and responsibly related. In this way we may help the reader to assess and make his or her own decisions in Church and society.

God's love and social structures

It is important that individuals should take the trouble to make their own decisions. No man may believe for another. Faith has a personal, existential dimension which requires personal commitment to action. Since however the life of the Christian is lived in society, there is an important social dimension which must be considered at every stage in the formulation of Christian ethics. Social responsibility is not an abstract concept which the Christian can carry around like an aura of sanctity. It can only be properly fulfilled within a society conscious of social responsibility, or within the framework of an attempt to create such a responsible society. I have written elsewhere of the role of the Church in society, both in terms of general considerations and in the context of the specific twin evils of poverty and racism in the world.[2] Something more could be said here about the basic framework for social ethics.

Much traditional Christian ethics has concerned itself with questions of responsibility to the state, which was seen as an order of creation, my country, my nation, my race. In Europe the experience of the last fifty years has made at least some theology more conscious of the dangers of the ecclesiastical undergirding of nationalism. One of the basic elements of this concept is the careful thinking through of the relation between freedom and responsibility in society. The freedom which comes as a gift of God is freedom to act for the good of one's fellow men. In the concept of the responsible society freedom and responsibility go together. In promoting the responsible society the proper attitude to war becomes, as we shall suggest, the constant positive maintenance of peace. This may be done, for example, by supporting moves towards the reduction of tension, by active resistance to a tendency to militarism, by social action to reduce differentials between the haves and the have-nots of the world, by resistance to all racialist policies.

God, Christians affirm, is a God of order and not of disorder. Traditional Catholic Christianity has often found great difficulty in breaking away from support of the established order of things in Church and state alike. Protestantism, on the other hand, has at times suffered from an institutional principle of the opposite kind. *Ecclesia semper reformanda:* the world turned upside down. The positive side of this tendency is liberty, the negative side is anarchy.

Christians are often a minority voice in modern society. As such, they may become involved in the politics of dissent or protest. Not every protest is well-judged, e.g. protests during the recent papal visit to Britain. For the sake of conscience, however, they may have to protest against a predominating power structure, to restrain totalitarian political power, to alter prevailing customs and values in a society. As conscientious objection, seeking to appeal to moral sensibility, such protest is usually non-violent and orderly. If progress is slow, and more direct methods are used, the risk of violence arises. When does direct action become the reckless use of power, an immoral act opposed to the basic intention of the creation of the responsible society?

In such a world of unclear possibility, where is the role of the Church? The Church is in the world, even if not of it. If it is part of the Christian task to proclaim and act out in commitment a foretaste of God's rule in men's hearts, then the Church will be a constant source of constructive criticism in society. The Church is concerned with persons, not as isolated individuals but in society. Where persons are treated as less than persons, Christians must actively oppose such treatment. Here is the Christian justification for active commitment to human rights and civil liberties. The state functions to preserve law and order. But where this cuts across the integrity and social integration of persons, Christians must protest in the name of God and of humanity, humanity as persons seen supremely in the person of Jesus Christ. (This is not, of course, an argument for individualism and free enterprise as political options as such, in opposition to a planned society.) Neither Church nor state *is* the kingdom of God. Both live in tension with each other and the kingdom. There will always be continuing tension between the actual justice achieved by the state (and by the Church) and the fullness of justice promised by the gospel of the love of God. This gospel not only serves as a norm for Christian critique of society. It is also the informing principle of social action which makes possible the transformation of social morality and the structure of justice in the political order.[3]

The sources of Christian ethics
What then is the basis of Christian ethics, individual and social, and what are the principles of decision making in areas of right and wrong? Most Christian ethical decisions involve, as we have seen, fundamental issues in moral philosophy. We cannot expect to find instant solutions to problems which have been debated for thousands of years, and which will no doubt continue to be the focus of attention for professional philosophers in the future. Christian ethics has always been a live subject, the focus of lively debate and discussion, and will continue to be so. We must make our own contribution at a particular place and time, grateful to be able to stand on the shoulders of those who have tackled similar issues in the past. This is not simply a matter of academic interest, for we are called to response in action now. We cannot wait for the perfection of principles in several thousand years' time! Too many theologians

spend their lives searching for the perfect theological method and failing to produce any kind of constructive theology. Such perfection is perfectly useless.

Different branches of the Christian tradition have looked back to different sources as keys to ethical reflection and action. In the modern world the differences within particular denominations are often more striking than those between different denominations, producing surprising agreements and differences in alignment.

Perhaps the obvious source of Christian ethics is the Bible, interpreted either exclusively as a self-contained book or inclusively with the aid of the Church's reflection on it through the ages. The Bible has sometimes in the past been seen as a book of rules, or as containing a book of rules for Christian conduct. These rules may be collated from such basic areas as the Genesis narratives of the garden of Eden, the ten commandments and the numerous lists of Old Testament prescription. Such codes, with suitable commentary, have been the basis of the Law in the Judaeo-Christian tradition. An obvious objection is that in the New Testament the law is overruled by the gospel. In some traditions, however, both Catholic and Protestant, Jesus is seen as the source of a new law which confirms and supplements the old. From this perspective, and with different combinations of the literal and the metaphorical in interpretation, different patterns of 'biblical ethics' may be obtained.

Sometimes there has been combined with this approach, again in both Protestant and Catholic traditions, a 'natural law' ethic, derived essentially from the mainstream of the Greek philosophical tradition and decisively stamped by the magisterial interpretation of St Thomas Aquinas. It is an interesting consequence of doctrinal development that some of the most consciously Protestant traditional ethical stances owe their existence to the implicit influence of St Thomas at an important stage in their development, usually in the seventeenth century.

More recent and characteristic of the 'new morality' of the present century is the ethic of '*agape*,' associated especially with the American theologian Joseph Fletcher. The basis is St Augustine's 'Love and do what you like.' So long as love is the motive and aim, all will be well. The central problem with such an approach is of course that even when we want to love, we do not always know what the most loving course of action is. For this reason we need rules to guide us in particular situations, rules based on the accumulation of previous experience.

Such reflection has suggested combination of an ethic based on laws, a 'prescriptivist ethic', and one based on *agape* alone. This is sometimes known as rule-agapeism, as distinguished from act-agapeism, in which one basically reacts to each new situation as it arises. We shall illustrate each of these approaches in relation to specific problems. My own approach is closest to the rule-agapeism model.

As I understand the matter, certain basic biblical themes have come to mould the life and character of the Christian community through the ages. Christians understand this process as taking place under the guidance of God. Reflection on the ethical content of this tradition includes question and reappraisal. The central themes of the tradition include appreciation of God as creator and reconciler, and of his hidden presence in sustaining grace in the created order. They include, too, the Christian understanding of the fulfilment of the Old Testament in the New, Jesus as the Christ, the preaching of the kingdom of God and the forgiveness of sins.

It is within this framework that we may understand God as in his essential nature self-giving love. Man is understood as created in the image of God, destined through Christ to reach a goal of new creation in a perfected relationship with God and his fellow men. Within this context of God, Father, Son and Spirit, a specifically Christian ethic may be developed. Without such a belief in God as the creator and reconciler of mankind, as sustainer of the universe, it is possible to build various general theories of ethics, but not to have a characteristically Christian ethic.

A good example of this close connection between theology and ethics can be seen in Karl Barth's last fragment on ethics on the Christian life. Here the problem of ethics is seen as part of the doctrine of reconciliation, and is set in the context of the Lord's prayer. The major themes, of childlikeness, of invocation, of God's sovereignty, carry frequent echoes of the main sections of his massive *Church Dogmatics*. Barth will certainly not provide answers to all our questions. For response to the complex questions raised by medical technology, for example, we may have to look at the careful work done in recent years in the United States. Barth's weakness, in declining to engage in dialogue with other disciplines in engaging in ethical issues, and in using the parabolic imagery of the Bible, is at the same time his great strength. Barth's ethics is everywhere an ethic of grace. Our freedom can only be genuine freedom in obedience to God, and in clear understanding of the distinction between the divine and the human. Human beings must strive for human justice, not for God's justice, which must be left to God. And we must pray for the coming of God's kingdom.

We must be able to maintain a proper distinction between the divine and the human, and to maintain a distinctively Christian ethic. At the same time, it is clearly important too for Christians to maintain a dialogue in thought and action with non-Christians in searching for ethical values, for the gospel is concerned with all mankind. Here we may perhaps reflect on some judicious comments from Professor Basil Mitchell. 'What matters is that the alternatives should be clearly and sympathetically presented, and that Christianity itself should be articulated and, more importantly, shown in such a way as to be a genuine option. Whether, in the long term, as the issues become clearer, there will be a movement predominantly towards Christian belief or away from our traditional ethic on the part of such reflective minds it is impossible to forecast. But Christianity has, throughout its history, displayed a regenerative power that justifies not only faith but hope.'

Summing up the argument of this chapter, we may say that Christians find the basis of characteristically Christian ethics in God himself. God is love, self-giving love. In his self-giving he has brought about the whole created order, and within creation has brought about new creation through Jesus Christ. Christians seek to be faithful in following the pattern of the character of Christ, reflected in the Bible and in Christian life and thought. This is the basis of concern for *all* mankind. Its working out in practice may involve rules and conventions and complex decisions, not as ends in themselves but in the service of all God's creatures.

Notes

1. There is a vast literature on ethics. Among recent philosophy in English we might mention the articles on ethics in *The Encyclopaedia of Philosophy*, ed. Paul Edwards, G.E. Moore's *Principia Ethica* (1903), Mary Warnock's *Ethics since 1900* (1960), W.D. Hudson's *A Century of Moral Philosophy* (1980) and W. Frankena, *Ethics* (1965). On the concept of justice see John Rawls' *A Theory of Justice* (1971). Christian ethics: On the principle of self-giving love, Gene

Outka's *Agape* can be highly recommended. See too,
K. Ward, *Ethics and Christianity* (1970), B. Hebblethwaite,
The Adequacy of Christian Ethics (1981), H. Smith and
L. Hodges, *The Christian and his Decisions* (1969), G.R. Dun-
stan, *The Artifice of Ethics* (1974), R.H. Preston. *Church and
Society in the Late Twentieth Century* (1983), James Gustavson,
Theology and Ethics (1981), Basil Mitchell, *Morality, Religious
and Secular* (1980). See too Peter Springer, *Practical Ethics*
(1979).
2. G.M. Newlands, *Theology of the Love of God* (1980), and
G.M. Newlands, *The Church of God* (1984).
3. On social ethics see too R.S. Downie and E. Telfer, *Respect
for Persons* (1969) and R.S. Downie, *Roles and Values*
(1971). The German periodical *Zeitschrift für Evangelische
Ethik* provides a journal for Christian social ethics at a very
high standard. There is nothing comparable in English.
On ethics and Church, Pannenberg's *Ethik und Ekklesiologie*
(1977) is illuminating. See too J. Habgood, *Church and
Nation in a Secular Age* (1983), and S. Hauerwas, *The
Peaceable Kingdom* (1983).

2. The Church and the Social Order

The very earliest Christian communities were concerned primarily with the Christian as an individual in relation to other members of the Christian community. Christianity was not a major social or political force, and Christians were not to be found in key positions of political power. This state of affairs meant that the Christian community tended to reflect the microcosm of Christian community rather than the macrocosm of world affairs. This has consequences for the interpretation today of New Testament material in relation to most specific issues in politics. Christians believe that Christ is the way, the truth and the life, and that God is the creator of the whole created order. They must then be concerned to relate their faith to all human activity and this includes the world of politics, which decisively shapes the lives of the population of our planet.

The whole question of the relation of Christianity to politics was raised sharply in the series of Reith Lectures on *Christianity and World Order* given by Dr Edward Norman, Dean of Peterhouse. In these lectures, which raised a great storm of protest, Dr Norman pointed unerringly to a number of fallacies in fashionable Christian responses to political issues. There is no doubt that certain causes become fashionable and even 'trendy'. They are taken up not only because of genuine ethical concern and desire to help those who are oppressed in various ways, but they also serve more dubious ends such as ecclesiastical party politics. So it

has been with issues like abortion and contraception, and
not least Christianity and politics.

These lectures criticized what was seen as an increasing tendency towards the politicization of Christianity.
This was reflected notably in the World Council of
Churches, in its pronouncements and in its grants to
liberation movements. There appeared to be a popular
left wing socialism endemic in theology. Coupled with
this politicization, equally evident and equally disastrous, was the naiveté and lack of political expertise
displayed by theologians and church leaders. These
charges were shrewd and intelligent. Indeed the large
scale indignation which the lectures provoked in Church
circles was to some extent a tribute to the accuracy of the
comments.

There were also contradictions. It is one thing to
draw attention to liberal sentimentality and fashionable
platitude. It is another matter to appear to ignore a
pressing need for reflection and action where human
beings are exploited. Dr Norman was critical of the
politicization of the faith. Yet his own proposals turned
out, far from being non-political, to be at least as far to
the right as those which he criticized were to the left.

The law

Christians, as St Paul never tired of telling his hearers,
are dead to the law and alive through the gospel of grace.
In Christian history this state of affairs has often given
rise to antinomianism, to the feeling that laws are
somehow an encumbrance of the old order, and Christians as individuals are somehow freed from such
constraints by the Spirit. A moment's reflection suggests
that the fabric of law is one of the most important
safeguards in almost every area of life. Bringing the law
into disrepute is often the prelude to dehumanizing
tendencies and totalitarian regimes.

We are thinking here not of church law but of the Church's understanding of the civil law. Just as the Christian thinker need not expect to be able to rewrite the philosophy of science, so he cannot expect to be able automatically, as a Christian, to contribute to the philosophy of law. His task is rather to reflect on the Christian understanding of humanity in God's creation. He will support such laws as contribute to the understanding of humanity in response to God's love, and oppose laws which restrict, exploit or destroy such humanity. This becomes a particularly acute problem in such areas as legislation concerning capital punishment.

On an individual level it is clear that the Christian as a citizen is under the same obligation as any other citizen to respect and obey the laws of the land. Even where laws may be regarded as unfair and inequitable, the appropriate procedure is not to break the law but to campaign for its alteration. Only in an extreme case may it be the Christian's particular duty to break the law, for example where humanity is being exploited, perhaps in a totalitarian regime which is completely impervious to the normal methods of persuasion by argument. Even in the Lutheran tradition, which has been much influenced by St Paul's argument in Romans that 'the powers that be are ordained by God', exceptions have usually been allowed. In Great Britain, in areas where the Church as an institution feels that it has a special interest, it has the opportunity to make its views known to the official parties and commissions on legal matters. Individual Christians who have been members of legislative assemblies or professional lawyers have of course made contributions which have stamped the character of law in different countries in decisive ways.

Political choice
The framing of legislation has a political as well as a legal

dimension. How is Christianity to be related to politics? It has been one of the most consistent complaints of recent liberation theology against classical Western theology that theologians have either been neglectful of the political dimensions of faith or else they have supported conservative and reactionary forces against the interests of the common people, either implicitly or explicitly: 'God bless the squire and his relations, and keep us in our proper stations!' There is always the twofold paradox in Christian life that we are both called out of the world in the service of God, and also called into the world. As citizens we have a duty to vote at elections for the political party which appears to offer the best programme for the government of our country. Our faith will guide us in this as in all else. Yet it is always difficult, if not impossible, to suggest that a Christian should vote for a particular political party. Christians are found in this country on all sides of the political divide. There have been, and there are, parties which have used the word 'Christian' in their title, like Christian Democrats. But there is no evidence that they have been more Christian than other parties. There are also political parties which most Christians would regard as proposing measures which are contrary to Christian principles. These would include parties which advocate racialist principles, like the National Front. We shall consider later the role of the 'German Christians' in Germany in the 1930s.

As we attempt to articulate our understanding of God's love as justice, we shall be forced to struggle to make the best political choices. In politics there are (often) grey areas, in which the best choice may be the lesser of two evils, or the best in the limitation of particular circumstances. How is a sensible solution to be reached without compromising either truth or love? This issue faces people in all areas of everyday life, and in

the realm of political choice most acutely. Are we to vote
for our own sectional interests, or for the common good?
What *is* the common good? How far can we speak of
making political choices for the good of humanity? Here
there arise the endless acute dilemmas between general
and special obligations which have been debated
throughout the history of moral philosophy. To what
extent should my obligations to my family come before
my obligations to my city, my country, to all mankind?
Should I buy British goods to keep my fellow country-
men in employment? Ought I rather to buy goods made
in third world countries where the need for trade is
infinitely greater? Should we keep down the price of
commodities like tea and cocoa in our country, so that
people on low incomes can afford them? Should we raise
the prices of such goods at home to produce a proper
living wage for workers in the countries where tea and
cocoa are produced? These are questions involving
political choices. They are also, as with many political
issues, closely tied with questions of economics. 'Money'
is not the favourite word on the lips of Christian
moralists. It is usually easier for us to talk of issues of a
more edifying nature. But if such problems as the use of
financial resources are ignored, then the Christian gospel
is clearly not served. Economics is a major social
science, and we shall return again to economic factors in
exploring specific issues in succeeding chapters.

The family
The role of the family in society, its impact on individual
lives and its place in wider social groups, is one of the
main themes of Christian ethics. The great development
of sociology in this century has produced large numbers
of case studies on patterns of family life.

Traditionally Christian life has often been seen in
terms of the life of the Christian family. There are many
good reasons to seek to strengthen family life. It is within

the natural affections of the family that love is given and exchanged from our earliest years. It is within families that we grow and develop as individuals and in relation to others. As we receive loving concern we develop the capacity to act in concern for others. Sometimes the history of Christian ethics, and indeed the history of our whole human community, can begin to appear as a record of problems, or uncertainty and conflict. There is, however, a much more positive side, in the vast reservoirs of affection and caring response given and received in human history. To ignore this enormous positive side of the human experience would be a great pity.

A number of factors in modern society have led to strain and tension in family life. Not least are the problems of poverty associated with unemployment which have caused endless bitterness, frustration and disillusionment. In such circumstances we shall obviously wish to support measures which add to the quality of family life and oppose factors which militate against.[1]

There are however, some qualifications which must be made to the affirmative principle. The family may come to have a constricting and destructive effect on human flourishing. For this reason some people have seen the dissolution of traditional family life as a cause for hope rather than despair. Many of the great novelists in history have shown the destructive effects of close family pressure on the lives of individuals over several generations. (In a similar way, close communities in towns and villages have had a corrosive effect on individual families). Not all family life is good for individuals. Love can be suffocating as well as liberating: all depends on the quality of the relationships.

In supporting the family we must not ignore the needs of others who are often socially less well off. Single people, one parent families, the widowed and the bereaved, all sorts of people may be actively neglected and set at a disadvantage by an insensitive concentration on the needs of the typical 'family'. Here as elsewhere in ethics, a concern for the right kind of balance is vital.

Employment

Much can be done for the quality of family life by cultivation and development of the traditional virtues of loving concern, patience and forbearance, consideration for the members of one's family in all areas of life. However, families are also very dependent on the social structures within which they live. Though there are undoubtedly wonderful instances in which hardship and deprivation bring people together, increasing the quality of human relationships, this fact is clearly no excuse for being complacent about social disadvantage in some sections of the population rather than others. Suffering and deprivation more often bring tension and bitterness which is destructive rather than creative of family life. When we speak of the fostering of the family we are not thinking of a restoration of 'Victorian values' or anything of the sort. We must think of employment, education and environment, of health care and the provision of housing at a price which people can afford, of a standard of living in which income keeps up with rising costs.

However politicians may cloak the figures, it is clear that there is in Britain in the 1980s a massive problem of unemployment. This brings tension in families and splits them up as they move around the country in the search for jobs.

Christian ethics identifies high unemployment as an area in need of urgent action. It cannot specify the details of the remedy. That is the task of the politician and the industrialist. There are no magic solutions. For example, simply to build factories to make equipment at a price that no one can pay, may be a short term measure but cannot provide help in the long term.

To consider unemployment is to raise again the question of employment, and the Christian understanding of the role and value of work, and more precisely of paid employment in society. Here we meet the fabled monsters of the Protestant work ethic, often thought to be characteristic of Calvinism, and the whole area of the relation of religion to the rise of capitalism. In reaction to the ethos of the Protestant work ethic, real or imagined, in which it is thought to be somehow a special Christian virtue that one should work as hard as possible for as long as possible in paid employment, there has grown up a new concern for a leisure ethic, in which the value of recreational activity is stressed A proper balance between work and leisure is always likely to enhance the quality of life. In a time of high unemployment such ideas acquire a new significance. Where people are valued in terms of what they do for a living, or even in terms of the salary they earn, this is a sad state of affairs. When employment ceases and the same people then cease to be valued and are looked down upon, it is disastrous. Even worse is the common result, that the unemployed may come to regard their condition as in some sense their own fault, become ashamed and lose their self-respect.

In such a position it is tempting to encourage people no longer to regard paid employment as a desirable goal, but to consider a permanent 'social wage' as a preferred option. Clearly in cases where there is no prospect of employment, it is important to help people to come to terms with this situation and to produce a creative response. Yet it seems to me that such a stance may often contain an undue element of idealism and unjustified optimism. As long as one part of a nation continues to provide good levels of economic opportunity and finan-

cial incentive it is not going to be prepared to move over
to a social wage philosophy offered by those who are
without work. There will remain the gap between those
who have and those who have not. All the destructive
tension created by gross inequality will remain.[2]

The inner city
Closely connected with employment is the whole large
question of social environment. In the flash points of civil
disturbance in modern Britain, in Northern Ireland, in
Liverpool, in Brixton, Bristol and elsewhere, high
unemployment has gone together with inner city decay.[3]
If the family is to be cherished, then its social environment has to be improved. Much has been heard of late of
environment in relation to ecology. Here there is often a
fundamental conflict of interest. The creation of green
belts, and the prohibition of all sorts of practices which
contribute to improving the physical or the animal
environment often have severe consequences for the
livelihood, housing etc. of the lowest income groups.
Hence the widespread feeling that 'environmentalism' is
a luxury that only the middle classes can afford. We can
hardly advocate the expenditure of large resources to
protect the natural environment at the expense of the
masses of people trapped in urban deprivation. Again a
careful balance has to be reached. Somehow resources
must be diverted to urban planning in such a way as to
produce a massive increase in the quality of life for the
poorest families. This must be achieved without flatten-
ing the national economy through punitive taxation, or
squandering millions of pounds in building the wrong
sort of council housing. Experience in Glasgow and
elsewhere has shown that this may create quite as many
problems as it solves, particularly if the quality of
construction is poor. Christian ethics is committed, as
befits a religion whose centre is the incarnation, to the

nuts and bolts of improving respect for persons as much by encouraging better standards of urban drainage as by purely philosophical discussion. Otherwise it can easily become a mere charade to enable the idle rich, or at least the comparatively rich, to pass the time of day without being engaged in the real issues of modern society.

We have just mentioned the rich and the comparatively rich. In Britain in recent years there has been observed the beginnings of a group in society described as an 'under class'. These people have none of the traditional benefits and values of the working man, and somehow lose out on almost all the positive advantages of modern society. Such people often come into conflict with the law, and suffer from all the negative aspects of police presence. They experience the degrading conditions which characterize prisons in Britain and in many other comparatively affluent countries.

When people consider the influence of Christian ethics upon the nation in modern times, it is the prison reformers like Elizabeth Howard, and the leaders of the campaign to abolish slavery like William Wilberforce who spring to mind, rather than the writers of books on moral theology in the period. For this there is much justification.

Housing and health
Closely connected with the social structure, and central to the quality of life in the family, are housing, health and education.

The question of housing is complicated by the fact that though more than half of the population of Britain buys its own houses, usually with the help of a building society mortgage, ownership is not evenly distributed around the country. Those who for a variety of good reasons are unwilling or unable to buy their homes are at a serious disadvantage. The provision of really adequate local authority housing is expensive. What is provided is all too often quite unsuitable. There is in any case nothing like the supply necessary in this country to meet the demand, while the plight of the homeless in the third world is often catastrophic. Many post–1945 developments such as high rise flats, though they would doubtless be considered luxurious by the inhabitants of the shanty towns of Latin America or South Africa, have been shown to give rise to all sorts of stress in communities and often to breakdown in mental health. Loneliness and isolation are among the main problems. Different political parties would apply different solutions to the housing problem. The Christian ethicist must point to the urgency of the issue, and to the need for action which will deal realistically with the actual situation at a given time.

Related to housing is the centrally important issue of national health care. We mentioned the problems of mental health which can arise in high rise flats. But inadequate housing strikes at physical health throughout the world. Again the sections of society who are socially most at a disadvantage are at the greatest risk to their physical health. There is a sort of 'Catch 22' world in which some sections of the population are at the bottom of all tables of desirable qualities of life. To enunciate lofty principles for ethics for an ivory tower world without reference to the real areas of deprivation and anguish would be inappropriate, not to say immoral. It is clear that comprehensive health care is extremely expensive and cannot be achieved without sacrifice in other areas of a national economy. The better off can purchase private facilities either as a 'topping up' of what government provides or as an alternative. But only a small proportion of families can afford this. Worse, it may be argued that private health insurance, like private education, diverts valuable resources away from general availability, masks problems and leads the governing classes to distance themselves and their families from the problem, and so to ignore it.

There is no need to attribute any special degree of wickedness or 'malice aforethought' to those whose decisions increasingly depress certain sections of society. It is much more often a case of 'out of sight, out of mind'. Where society is increasingly polarized there is less and less immediate contact between its various sections. It may be, too, that a higher standard of living breeds a certain optimism, and so the quite desperate plight of thousands of citizens in this country and millions throughout the world is ignored. There is a great grey area here of half guilty ignorance, acquiescence with compromise, in which the Churches have little excuse, and yet are very easily involved.

Health is then intimately related to such matters as housing and to economic standards generally. We shall come shortly to other areas of medicine, and here too it is important to bear the entire health perspective in mind. It is comparatively easy to bring together thousands of supporters of an organization to campaign against abortion at Hyde Park Corner. It is much more difficult to mobilize Christians to seek action on a situation in which thousands of old people die of hypothermia every winter because they can't afford to keep themselves warm. Some causes become fashionable, others do not. Christian ethics needs to be aware of these temptations.

Education and poverty
Education is one of the main dimensions of family life. Where there is the possibility of educational training to develop the full potential of human culture and intellect, the family may flourish. Where such opportunities are denied, limited and in various ways frustrated, tensions arise which affect the welfare of the family over all areas

of life and over a number of generations. Since Christians are concerned to become instruments of God's love to his people in society, they cannot be satisfied with an educational system which may bring advantages to some sections of a community while being disadvantageous to others. Christians can scarcely pronounce on the best philosophies of education and the best ways of putting these into practice. They *are* however committed, in understanding love as fairness to all, to working to ensure equality of opportunity as far as possible for all families, in education. Such a principle will bring to the minds of readers in Britain the advantages and disadvantages of educational facilities in this country. Looked at on a global scale however, it becomes clear how very far we are from even the most minimal fulfilment of a Christian understanding of the provision of education. We have hardly even begun to cope with the problems of hunger and starvation, and we cannot expect children to respond to education where they are hungry, and where there is no prospect of opportunity to use such education as they may acquire. Again it becomes clear that all these ethical issues are inextricably related. They may have to be distinguished and tackled separately, but we cannot resolve one problem without progress in related areas. The effects of disadvantage in these areas have been well documented for Liverpool by David Sheppard in his *Bias to the Poor*. Poverty and racial discrimination often go together.

Poverty affects the whole of a society, and it becomes a way of living. It then leads to greater poverty. Opportunities narrow and the whole becomes a vicious circle. Clearly it is no part of the Christian gospel to attempt to save souls and maintain them in squalor. If we ask why poverty still exists in societies where there are the economic resources to eliminate it, then the Christian will see the root cause in the sin of humanity in general.

Alienation from God leads men to build institutional structures to secure their possessions, and to exclude those who are economically weaker. Alienated from co-humanity man is increasingly alienated from himself, and the notion of service to his fellow men in time disappears.

If poverty is to be reduced, specific conditions must be created, through the creation of employment, training for work, improvement of living conditions and facilities for social work. All depends not only on the will to plan but on willingness to implement the programmes. The Christian believes that this is ultimately possible when alienation is overcome through the gracious love of God.[5]

Poverty is often bound up with racism. Racism is itself the product of a strange neurosis, an expression of social disintegration designed to relieve a sense of guilt and to establish self respect. As such it damages the racist as much as his victim. Racism is a form of idolatry to which Christians must be opposed without qualification. Yet it must be said that this has not been the case in many instances in the twentieth century, in German Christian theology, in racism in South Africa, in America and elsewhere, not least in the disturbing failure to provide true equality for the minority races and the new immigrants in Britain.

What has been said of racism applies with equal force to all kinds of religious intolerance, for example of the sort seen constantly in Northern Ireland. It applies to discrimination against minorities of all sorts. Much has been written in recent years on women's rights, and we shall not go into detail here. We may note however the connection between prejudice and poverty. Women have historically been paid much less than men, and their employment opportunities are still much more limited. This is an area in which the Churches' record is hardly impressive. I have written of this elsewhere, and make no further comment here except to affirm that I personally very much doubt the theological propriety of pleading the exigencies of sacramental theology against the basic principles of Christian ethics in considering the role of women in the Christian community.

In summing up the problem of the relation of the Church to the social order I would like to stress again two large areas in which the shape of the issues has been transformed in recent years. The first area is that of economic development. Of course economic issues have always deeply affected people's lives. But here the interdependence of one nation upon another has sharply increased in the last few decades. Social policies aimed at the realization of moral goals, are affected by such matters as the fluctuation of interest rates in money markets thousand of miles away from the scene of their application. Western Europe is notoriously dependent on what happens in the United States. In considering issues in social ethics Christians must be careful of espousing simple solutions which founder when faced with the complex interrelationships in economic reality.

The second major issue is the development of the whole relation of society and religion in human culture. The last two decades have seen the growth of secularization in various forms on the one hand, and of strongly fundamentalist revivals in the major world religions on the other hand. There have been numerous exceptions to the rules. In Western academic communities, for example, the general secularizing refraction of analytic philosophy has had important exceptions, in the considerable number of British philosophers who have espoused and defended traditional Catholic theology. But these cases are all the more striking for being exceptions. More widely there has been a considerable decline in religious belief throughout Europe and America, in France and Italy as much as in England and

Scandinavia; and in sharp contrast to all of this the revival of Islam, of 'born again' Christianity and of traditional popular Catholicism. This colourful contrast serves to underline the irreducibly plural nature of modern society, a pluralism which seems likely to increase, unless crushed by the physical imposition of some totalitarian scheme of thought.

There is then for Christians in community a standing obligation to be active in raising the quality of provision in the social structures of society. This obligation arises, not from a sense of guilt or emotional reaction, but as a basic positive commitment to liberating men and women from the constraints of social disadvantage, which prevent them from living to the full in the freedom of the children of God for which God has created them.

Notes

1. David Brown says of industrial disputes that 'Quite often, the most appropriate interpretation of them is that they are an expression of the dignity of the worker, with questions of justice only nominally having the dominant role' (*Choices*, 74f).
2. From the *Reply to E.R. Norman* we may mention David Jenkins' chapter, 'Doctrines which drive one to politics'. cf.p.150f. 'If Christ died for all men, then you cannot write off increasing political awareness as simply liberal or trendy nonsense.' cf. also his Durham Enthronement Sermon, September 1984.
3. Cf. David Sheppard, *Bias to the Poor*, 49f. 'My experience has been that working class people in east and south-east London are not helped by clergy and congregation to believe that Christ could be for them. It is certainly true that they want to know that church people have deep spiritual roots; but their interest disappears if they discover that there is no willingness to be involved in issues which reflect the quality of life of the whole community. It is their

complaint that they have not seen a bias for the poor reflected consistently in the Churches'. Sheppard stresses the vulnerability of black people in our society. cf. too *'Geoff': the life of Geoffrey M. Shaw*, by R. Ferguson, Glasgow, 1979.

4. In his excellent essay on *Catholicism and World Order* of 1979 (Catholic Institute for International Relations), Professor Michael Dummet says this of Dr Norman's argument (p.8f). 'He seems to think it is the poor and the oppressed who are being called on to redeem themselves from their own poverty and their own oppression.... But he is quite wrong: those who are being called on to end the manifold and bitter oppression of human beings that disfigures our world are not those who suffer it, but those who are responsible for it and have the power to end it. It is true that Christ did not teach the poor to clamour for the goods of the rich; but he told the rich young man to distribute these goods.'

5. The 1984 miners' strike showed how extremism in the leadership on both sides leads to tragic conflict and hardship in the communities most affected.

3. Peace and War in a Nuclear Age

War, contrary to some popular belief, is not simply an invention of the overfed European middle classes to serve as an outlet for their surplus energy and a means of keeping down the peasantry in an age innocent of effective means of contraception. I understand that in prehistoric times – though I cannot speak from first-hand experience – competition for pasture and grazing lands led nomadic tribesmen to continual skirmishes. Such conflicts frequently had theological implications, particularly among head-hunters, for whom the head as the seat of the soul had magic powers and was well worth collecting. For some the severed head was seen as an image of the moon and so a symbol of fertility. The victim should be beheaded from the back to the front and not vice-versa, so that the setting up of a personal relationship through looking each other in the eye might be avoided. I-thou relationships would appear to be a prominent part of stone-age culture.

Wars then came naturally to be assessed by all the major religions of mankind, and were often held to be justified. Christianity developed the theory of the just war. Aztec religions held wars to be legitimate. Confucianism's support of war increased as it advanced to becoming a state religion. Buddha was a supporter of non-violence. Later Buddhism got the best of both worlds by allowing the less highly initiated to fight and defend the full members of the sacred community, thus permitting the latter to remain undefiled from the taint of

war. We shall encounter this logic again. In Islam a high
incidence of nomadic culture coupled with a strong faith
in predestination often led to a favourable attitude to
war. Evidence of this sort, backed up by many years of
research, led the distinguished student of comparative
religion, Joachim Wach, to this general conclusion.
Religions like early Buddhism which were convinced of
the fallen state or unreformable character of the world
were disinclined to wars, and particularly to wars of
religion. Religions like Islam, which believed in the
improvement of the world if only it had the right sort of
religion, tended to go in for religious wars of conquest.[1]

In Greece, Homer and the poets could sing the praises
of war and the warrior. On the other hand, they all
looked back to the golden age of peace when there had
been no wars, and hoped for its return. If there had to be
violence, said Plato, then the amount of violence used
should be the minimum required to get satisfaction from
the enemy (*Republic*, 469–71). Justice for Plato was
giving every man his due. From here it was only a step to
Aristotle's definition of the just war as a war whose
object was to enslave those designed by nature for
servitude, but who resisted their proper assignment on
the social scale. (*Politics* 1.1256B, 23–26). This convention was taken over in Roman theory of war. Cicero
stressed the important addition that any war, to be just,
must be waged by the state (*De Officiis* I, 34–40, 83; II
27:III 46, 107). As he puts it in a nutshell, individuals
die, but the state should live for ever (*De Republica* 3.34).

Bible and tradition
In the Old Testament, in the earliest period, Jahweh
himself wages Israel's wars. (Ex.14.4f.; Deut.1.10;
Josh.10.14f. etc.) When the ark of the covenant is
brought into the camp, then Jahweh the warrior is
present (Ex.15.3 and I Sam.4.3f.) and the war may

become a holy war (I Sam.21.5f.; Isa.13.3; Jer.22.7). The people of God consecrate themselves, the sacred oracle says, 'Jahweh has given x into your hands'. The people of God are now certain and march into battle without fear, trusting in God. The enemy are terrified, the cry of battle arises, the judgement of God is executed on the enemy and God's verdict is carried out on the defeated. With the rise of the kingdom strategic considerations begin to outweigh those of holy war. Now David, not Jahweh himself, leads Jahweh's wars. Political and diplomatic considerations play a greater role. The old idea of the holy war of the Lord is now carried on by the prophets, whose message takes on an increasingly eschatological colouring. Jahweh's day of battle will break upon the people (Isa.34; Zeph.1.7f.), will kill the heathen and bring final salvation to Israel.

The concept of the final victory of God over his enemies is equally familiar to the New Testament, but here victory is tied up finally with the mission of Jesus (Mark 3.24–7; John 16.33f.; Luke 10.18) in the gospels, and with the cross and the exaltation of Christ in St Paul (Rom.8.37f.). There are numerous references to swords, force, soldiers and Caesar, but there is nothing which amounts to an unqualified legitimation of war.[2] On the other side, there are the famous texts from the sermon on the mount. Resist not evil, turn the other cheek, go the second mile, love your enemies. As St Paul puts it (Rom.12.19), 'My dear friends, do not seek revenge, but leave a place for divine retribution'. Clearly, if Chillingworth was right in affirming that 'The Bible, I say, and the Bible only, is the religion of Protestants', then the problems are considerable.

What was the attitude of the early Christian communities to war and peace? There is a widespread belief that in the early Church there was a classical time, like Homer's golden age of peace in the past, in which

Christians were united in faith and love and to a man would have nothing to do with war. Followers of gentle Jesus meek and mild, the nearest they would have got to a uniform, would have been a prototype for Salvation Army attire. It was only with the coming of establishment that good Christians were seduced into more worldly ways of thought by the powers that be. Today a breaking away from the establishment may herald a return to the innocent days of yore. So Donald Mackinnon, in *The Stripping of the Altars*: 'Although it is late, desperately late in the day, one may hope that in the post-Constantinian age the Churches will be able to turn their energies again to serious engagement with the problems raised by war. Where England is concerned, the passing of establishment as we know it would surely lead to a day in which episcopal lawn sleeves would cease to flutter in the breeze as their wearer bestowed the diocesan blessing upon the latest Polaris submarine.'

Others, no advocates of establishment, like Helmut Gollwitzer, have regarded the notion of a classical time of total abstention from war by Christians as a legend. The best account of the early position has come to us from Hans von Campenhausen, himself a leading liberal opponent of Nazi militarism. Some Christians were probably soldiers from fairly early times.[3] There was no consensus of opinion and no occasion for a common declaration. Most Christians were probably not involved in affairs of state and in the army for purely sociological reasons. As the Letter to Diognetus indicated, they thought of themselves as strangers to the world, and this applied to most of the world's activities, including war. None doubted that in the world wars must be fought (Tertullian, *Apology*, 30, Cyprian, *To Demetrianus*, 20, Arnobius, *Adv.Nat.*4.36). But they wanted to keep out of it (Justin, *Dialogue* 110). When Tertullian says (*De Corona* 11) that 'every uniform is forbidden among us, because it is the distinguishing mark of a profession which is not allowed' the main object of his fear is not the activity of the soldier as such but the fear of cultic pollution through involvement with heathen military worship. Even a bishop, as in the case of Paul of Samosata, might have his own escort of spear bearers (Eusebius, *Eccles.Hist.* 7,30,8). Celsus asked why Christians took the protection of the state without sharing in the burden of its defence, to which Origen replied that the Christian's contribution was to pray for the Emperor. But, what would happen when all the empire was Christian? Who would defend it then? What happens when the Emperor himself becomes a Christian? Is he to defend the state by force of arms?

The turning point indeed came with Constantine, though not for the reasons often adduced. Constantine brought back into the army those Christians who had been thrown out by Diocletian in 314 at the Council of Arles, and promoted them. The Church pronounced its anathema on every deserter from the army. Athanasius, in his *Epistola ad Amunem*, says that the killing of one's enemies, though normally forbidden, is in war not only permitted but praiseworthy. In 416, Theodosius II issued a decree to the effect that from henceforth only Christians should be allowed to enter the army. Cyprian says of killing 'it is called a virtue, when it is done in the public interest' (*Ad Donatum*, 6) and Ambrose (*De Officiis* 1.29) praises the courage of soldiers who fight for their country. Firmicus Maternus, in his *On the errors of pagan cults*, appeals to the emperors Constans and Constantius to destroy pagan temples by force and protect the Christian shrines. Augustine (*The City of God*, 19.7) takes up and affirms the Ciceronian distinction between the just and the unjust war. (This incidentally had already been criticized by Origen, *Contra Celsum*.4.82; 8.73.)

So, inch by inch, the process goes on. The middle ages only clarified the regulations for the just war. War must be waged by a lawful authority, for a just cause, with the intention of eventual peace. A just cause involved, of course, the struggle against heathen and heretics, especially in the holy wars of the crusades. In the development of moral theology war could be made one of the duties of the vassal to God as well as to man. Absolution could be guaranteed and martyrs' crowns promised to the fallen, and the duty to fight in the interest of the Church generally reinforced.

Love does not preclude a benevolent severity, said Augustine, nor that correction which compassion itself dictates. St Thomas followed Augustine, Aristotle and Cicero: a just war requires the authority of the prince, a just cause, and a correct intention, i.e. of promoting good and avoiding evil. The Renaissance brought, on the one hand, Machiavelli's open contempt for religious scruples and sanctions save for diplomatic purposes, and on the other, the humanism of Erasmus, with his Complaint of Peace. 'The Lord's Prayer addresses our Father, but how can they call upon a common Father who drive steel into the bowels of their creatures? Christ was a shepherd of sheep, Christians tear each other like wolves.'

It is worth pursuing the story further, as we see how, like layers of paint on a canvas, a venerable and apparently natural tradition develops, with differences in detail but with the broad landmarks always in increasingly familiar places, until anything else would seem awkward and indeed grotesque. In his doctrine of the two kingdoms, Martin Luther distinguished between public office and private person. The call of Jesus for love without violence is binding for the life of the individual. But he may also with a good conscience, participate in public life, in which violence is unavoidable. The Christian participates with both hands in the double rule of the world by God the preserver of creation and God the redeemer. For Calvin the most important statement is at *Institutes* 4.20.10f. 'How can magistrates be pious men and shedders of blood at the same time. It is not for the pious to afflict or to hurt; yet to avenge, at the Lord's command, the afflictions of the pious is not to hurt or to afflict.... I say that an express declaration of this matter is not to be sought in the writings of the apostles; for their purpose is not to fashion a civil government, but to establish the spiritual kingdom of Christ.' One might feel that a process of demythologizing is here already in train!

The pacifist position was left to the unfortunate and ruthlessly hunted Anabaptists. It was particularly the Enlightenment, weary of religious intolerance, which highlighted the defects of the just war theory through scorn. Kant in his pamphlet of 1795, *On Perpetual Peace*, condemned the just war because he thought it could never succeed in being just. None used satire to more effect than Mark Twain. 'O Lord our God, help us to tear their soldiers to bloody shreds with our shells. Blast their hopes, water their way with tears, stain the white snow with the blood of their wounded feet. We ask it in the spirit of love, of him who is the source of love, and who is the very-faithful refuge and friend of all who are sore beset and seek his aid with humble and contrite hearts. Amen.' In Russia Tolstoy, standing in the monastic tradition of the kenotic Christ, became a symbol of pacifism throughout the literate world.

The First World War brought the issue again to a head. The Bishop of London, Winnington-Ingram, had no doubts. 'As I have said, I look upon it as a war for purity, I look upon everyone who dies in it as a martyr.' The ninety-three German intellectuals sent their telegram of support to the Kaiser. In Switzerland the youthful Karl Barth had other views. 'The absolute ideas of the gospel are being simply suspended until further notice, and German war theology is put in their place, christianized with a lot of talk about "sacrifice" and the like.'[4] The mood in the second war was in general, much more sober. Bonhoeffer's adaptation of a Luther illustration catches the feeling well. 'When a madman is tearing through the streets in a car, I, as a pastor who happens to be on the scene, must do more than merely console or bury those who have been run over, I must jump in front of the car and stop it.' The coming of the nuclear age, to which we must give special attention, added a new dimension, early recognized as decisive. By 1948, the World Council of Churches had come round to the unequivocal declaration that 'war is against the will of God', and even such an arch-conservative as Cardinal Ottaviani could affirm that war is entirely forbidden by God.

A couple of examples will illustrate the gap between the theory and practice of war. Typical of the Reformed position is the following from the Westminster Confession: 'God, the supreme Lord and King of all the world, hath ordained civil magistrates to be under him over all the people, for his own glory, and the publick good; and, to this end, hath armed them with the power of the sword, for the defence and encouragement of them that are good, and for the punishment of evil-doers. It is lawful for Christians to accept and execute the office of a magistrate, when called thereunto; in the management whereof, as they ought especially to maintain piety, justice and peace, according to the wholesome laws of each commonwealth; so, for that end, they may lawfully, now under the New Testament, wage war upon just and necessary occasions.'

(Westminster Confession, XXIII, Of Civil Magistrates, paras 1 and 2. There is appended a selection of New Testament citations.)

The Church has spoken. The matter is closed. After all, anything that goes on 'now, under the New Testament' must be entirely proper. But what do you mean by war? The truth is always concrete.

'All five men shot, but Eriksson aimed his weapon – a grenade launcher, which looks like a shotgun – down into the valley, away from the general direction of Mao. In addition, Rafe flatly said, "Eriksson stated, 'Oh no', like he regretted that he had fired." Rafe himself let go with a burst from his M–16, which, inexplicably, caused his rifle to jam. However, he did call Clark's attention to a bush directly ahead. It was rustling. "I couldn't tell whether it was Charlie (Vietcong) or the girl." Rafe testified. Clark, who was several metres in front of Rafe, yelled back to him that it was the girl. "I saw him raise his rifle," Rafe stated, adding that he then started moving towards Clark. Moving in on the bush, Clark started blazing away with his M–16, and at once the rustling foliage grew still. "You want her gold tooth?" Clark called over his shoulder to Rafe, who was then, as he testified, a foot away and was staring, aghast, at Mao. "When I got up to the girl, I saw that her head was partially blown away," he testified. "She was dead, I'm sure."' (*The Observer*, 16 November 1969, from Vietnam.)

It may be helpful to summarize briefly the position described so far.

1. Many different attitudes to war and peace, some of them mutually contradictory, are to be found both within the Bible itself and in the history of Christian thought.

2. Early Christianity, living as a small enclave in the midst of society, was able to a large extent, to abstain from the adoption of political stances in society, and so reached no consensus regarding peace and war.

3. The gradual development of Christendom, following the Constantinian settlement, led to the development of the Christian theory of the just war, which drew heavily on classical and Old Testament models.

4. The Reformation continued the medieval practice but

modified its theological foundation in various ways.

5. A radical pacifism was adopted only by the left wing of the Reformation, to some extent with the aid of ideas derived from the late medieval sects.

6. Modern critical attitudes to the traditional Christian attitude to war stem historically from the Quakers and from the Enlightenment.

7. It is generally recognized that the recent development of weapons capable of destroying the human race calls for a radical reappraisal of the problems of war and peace.

Peace movements

Before taking up the implications of this survey, I ought to say something about *peace* movements in the history of Christian thought. These arose in the Middle Ages out of the *devotio moderna*, the brothers of the common life in Holland, and from the Cathari, the Waldensians, and other small groups who tried to live by vigorous adherence to the sermon on the mount. Along with this, and in Holland at least, connected with it, came the renaissance emphasis on *humanitas* and the development of the concept of toleration, in the work of Erasmus, John Colet and Thomas More. Anabaptists stressed the command to love as a law, seeking not social renewal in the world but the realization of the fruit of justification within the community of believers. All Anabaptists were condemned to death by Catholics and Protestants combined at the Diet of Speyer in 1529, and in 1542 alone 2173 of them were executed. The same spirit was shown by the Mennonites in America, the Quakers in England, and the Molokan monks in Russian Orthodoxy. In his essay, 'Towards the present and future peace of Europe' (1693), the Quaker William Penn proposed, among other things, the setting up of a European parliament. The seventeenth and eighteenth centuries saw the publication of numerous 'plans for universal peace', particularly in France. Then came the balance of power theories of the restoration in Europe and the Holy Alliance. The early nineteenth century saw the formation of small pacifist groups, often of Quaker origin, which were instrumental in the setting up of peace conferences at The Hague, out of which came the Hague Convention. 1864 brought the foundation of the Red Cross. But the national churches made little contribution to all this till the Amsterdam meeting of the World Council of Churches in 1948. Since then numerous organizations have been set up, religious and non-religious, which have sought to create a climate of opinion in which peaceful, rather than warlike, intentions will be encouraged. Their success can only be judged by later generations, if there are any.

The twentieth century

The coming of the nuclear age forced people to think again about the conventional wisdoms of war and peace. But the revelation of the full scale of the devastation created in the First World War, and its social aftermath, had already created a sober mood. Emil Brunner, writing in 1932 in his influential *The Divine Imperative*, felt obliged to repeat that 'to deny, on ethical grounds, the elementary right of the state to defend itself by war, simply means to deny the existence of the state itself'. But he went on to say that, 'if war were to break out at the present time, it is extremely uncertain whether the idea of fighting in defence of one's country, would have any meaning at all. War has outlived itself. To expect to establish any just order by means of a world conflagration – called war – has become a political madness.' He called for the further development of international law.[5]

Such a humane Christian approach sounded and was eminently reasonable, and quickly became the new

conventional wisdom. The consequences were disastrous, as Hitler used the reluctance to fight as an
opportunity to enslave most of Europe. In America the
seeds of a new perspective were sown in Reinhold
Niebuhr's *Moral Man and Immoral Society*, and in *An
Interpretation of Christian Ethics*. There are echoes here of
Luther's two kingdoms. 'All social grouping on a larger
scale than the most intimate social group requires a
measure of coercion.' Pacifism of Tolstoy's sort simply
prolonged the subjection of the weakest social classes.
Love need not preclude a realist and pragmatic approach
to problems. Liberal Christianity denied the reality of
evil in the hope of a triumph of love. Orthodoxy saw
order as a remedy for sin, and so denied justice. Niebuhr
affirmed both 'the relevance of an impossible ethical
ideal' and the need to establish justice through a realist
approach to politics. Justice is impossible without
forgiveness. 'Nothing short of the knowledge of the true
God will save men from the impiety of making themselves God and the cruelty of seeing their fellow men as
devils, because they are involved in the same
pretensions.[6]

Brunner had relied for his ethical structure on the
Lutheran doctrine of 'orders of creation'. Niebuhr
objected strongly. 'There must be something in the order
of creation which makes it normative. But it is difficult to
find this normative principle because man is an historical
creature and there are no purely "natural" forms in his
life which have not been submitted to both the freedom
and the corruption of history.' Against Brunner then it
may be said that from a Christian point of view the good
is defined not by what is early, late, rational or natural,
but by what is good for man in a given situation. On the
other hand, you can plunge on with Niebuhr, aware of
your sinfulness, but using force to bring about justice in
the ambiguities and complexities of a situation in which

there is neither black nor white but an endless sea of grey. Here, too, are pitfalls. We must look for better guides.

Dietrich Bonhoeffer in his *Ethics* (1942) was still hopeful about Western civilization. Western wars have always distinguished between means of warfare which are permissible and right, and those which are prohibited and criminal. It is only when Christian faith is lost that man must himself make use of all means, even criminal ones, in order to secure by force the victory of his cause. In writing of 'the right to bodily life', Bonhoeffer, seeking a recovery of the concept of 'the natural' in Protestant thought, writes that 'the first right of natural life consists in the safeguarding of the life of the body against arbitrary killing. One must speak of arbitrary killing wherever innocent life is deliberately destroyed. This means that the killing of the enemy in war is not arbitrary killing.' Here we have the crucial question. Is the entire population on the 'other side' to be regarded as the enemy? Again Bonhoeffer follows the Lutheran tradition. All killing in war is sinful, but may be forgiven through Jesus Christ. At the same time Bonhoeffer was, of course, making his own contribution to the struggle against Hitler, for which he was to pay with his own life.

If we want to consult an independent thinker on theology we are not often disappointed by Karl Barth, whatever we may think of his advice. 'The problem of avoiding war is present and has always to be tackled during every time of peace.' There is no point in shutting the stable door after the horse has bolted. Pacifism has 'almost everything to be said for it, and it is almost overwhelmingly convincing.' It should be impossible to do what the tradition has done and regard war as a normal element in the constitution of the state as part of the divine order. 'The normal, the crucial condition is that of peace'. The Church must involve itself directly in bringing about peace between people, and in educating the young against enthusiasm for war. Radical pacifism is a mistake because 'man can only take a relative decision'.[7] There might be an extreme circumstance in which a people has serious grounds for not allowing the loss of its independence. The decision must be a concrete one in a given case rather than a decision in principle. Which grounds for not allowing the loss of independence are sufficiently serious Barth cannot tell us, in principle.

The idea that theology, ethics and, in particular, war, can only be done and decided within a particular context has become the main theme of recent study in ethics. Now ethical criteria will arise out of the given situation. This line of approach could lead Paul Lehmann to conclude that 'in these terms Hiroshima and Nagasaki are signs of God's pressure towards a global implementation of the full humanity of man and to that extent are ethically significant and defensible'.[8] All very difficult. The contextual approach develops further in Joseph Fletcher's *Situation Ethics* into the question of what is fitting, rather than right or good, in relation to love. But that, of course, is *the* main dilemma. We need guidance on how to be loving. Once again the nuclear question raises the sharpest moral conflict. Paul Tillich wrote that 'one can never start an atomic war with the claim that it is a just war, because it cannot serve the unity of the kingdom of God. But one must be ready to answer in kind, even with atomic weapons, if the other side uses them first. The threat itself could be a deterrent.'[9] What is the connection between threat of global annihilation, deterrent and the love of God?

The peace of God
Ethics that claims to be Christian ethics has to face squarely and constantly the life and message of Jesus, his

preaching of the kingdom of God and his initiation of the process of the coming of the kingdom in his own life. Blessed are the peacemakers; God shall call them his sons. How blest are you, when you suffer insult and persecution and every kind of calumny for my sake. Accept it with gladness and exultation, for you have a rich reward in heaven; in the same way they persecuted the prophets before you. You have learned that they were told, 'Love your neighbour, hate your enemy'. But what I tell is this. Love your enemies and pray for your persecutors. Only so can you be the children of your heavenly Father. What would it be like to love? In the New Testament it would include looking after the prostitutes and the tax gatherers, the lepers and the outcasts, in the pattern of taking up the cross. The shape of the kingdom is the shape of the parables of the Good Samaritan and of the prodigal son.

If we take the sermon on the mount literally then its realization by us appears impossible in modern society. Indeed it appears to ignore the vital functions of law and planning in modern society. We may make distinctions between natural law and special grace, or between God the preserver and God the redeemer, but then we are back trying to serve two masters. It may be more helpful to try to understand the New Testament evidence rather as indicators pointing to and promising new possibilities.

It is always, of course, possible to leave the use of force and of law to non-Christians. But we all participate in the benefits of the social order. In any case, the gospel is for all mankind. If we decide to opt into politics and law, then we shall have to agree that love and some sort of force are not incompatible. We may come to argue that Christians, like police on the side of law and order, may participate in war to maintain that order in society which is necessary for survival. But there is a vital difference. For policemen killing is the last remedy: in war it comes first on the list. The final appeal is not to law but to force.

If the decision is made that a Christian may participate in war as a last resort, then the first decision must not involve an automatic legitimation of all and any methods. All methods of preventing war must first be tried and continued. Participation does not rule out the deepest personal abhorrence of violence.

It might be thought, however, that the reality in the 1980s rules out war completely. As more states acquire nuclear weapons, the danger of world annihilation increases. Even in a supposedly justifiable war there could be no justice left to preserve. Against this thesis may be set the numerous arguments suggesting the tactical use of nuclear weapons in limited stages of war. In the face of complete lack of experience of such wars, it is impossible to predict consequences with certainty. Even here there are important grades of activity. It is clearly better to destroy military bases than centres of civilian population. It is clearly better to build nuclear shelters, if we may assume that they may give some degree of protection, than to pursue a policy which deliberately solves the problem of emergency food supply by ensuring that fifty per cent of the population will not survive an initial attack.[10]

Whatever we may think necessary in an extreme situation, there can be no doubt that any policy which results in the destruction of people is in total discord with the love of God, and any policy which involves mass destruction is literally abhorrent beyond words.

If war is the immediate issue, then the wider horizon must always be peace. Blessed are the peacemakers, for they shall be called the sons of God. God is a God not of disorder, but of peace. Peace, we often feel, smacks of Utopia. Conflicts are a sign of a healthy society. The desire for coalitions has always been the downfall of politics. In a world dictatorship there would be no possibility of war. Clearly not every kind of peace is desirable. We may think of Plato's Republic, Calvin's Geneva or Stalin's Russia. The balance of terror is not peace. But conflicts produce progress in society only within a certain range, where certain general interests are observed. Progress now becomes an ethical task of the first importance.

The coming of the nuclear age is the fruit of recent progress in science and technology. It was a group of scientists who first raised with urgency the ethical problems involved in nuclear warfare. What matters now is the development of awareness of responsibility among scientists, the relation of scientific methods to human problems. This is the situation in which we must seek a renewed understanding of the way of peace.[11]

Peace in the Old Testament is the gift and the destiny which God gives to creation. Peace comes from God, bringing salvation. 'Nation shall not lift up sword against nation, neither shall they learn war any more.' In the New Testament, Christ is our peace. Peace in community becomes visible as the love of our neighbour, and it goes further than the Christian community. The sign of the transformation of the Christian is that he loves his enemy. This does not guarantee actual reconciliation, because the enemy is not himself free to accept love, but it is a step towards peace. Love changes the world, but does not pretend to bring it to perfection.[12]

Peace as God's final salvation acts upon Christian attitudes in the present. There will be conflicts in any peace that we can make. In politics we need to develop forms of reconciliation in which conflicts do not get out of control. Hope should free us from being entrapped in the present, opening possibilities before they can be seen. If modern society is to survive it needs peace. It must avoid the fanaticism of coerced utopias. It cannot afford the empty delusion of a papering over the cracks. The

Christian response to God and the world seeks to anticipate God's coming peace. We may hope to change the world by attention to detail rather than in magic transformation, for we may leave the changing of the whole to God. We may hope to be guided by principles rather than sets of rules, yet detailed rules for detailed cases may be the method on appropriate occasions.

Peace in Christian understanding is the salvation of God which shall come to the whole of his creation at the end of time. As we wait for it, we know that it has come already. As we know that we cannot create it, we should perhaps be released from the inhibitions which make it impossible for us to make peace.

Decisions

In the last few years there has grown up an enormous literature on nuclear war, which it would be impossible to assess adequately without considering the world strategic balance in detail. However, the main issues can be at least mentioned. I have indicated that I do not myself accept absolute pacifism, nor do I think that the theory of the just war is automatically acceptable. There is *almost* everything to be said for pacifism, and so the particular circumstances in which war is contemplated must be considered in each case with extreme care. The only reason for justifying a limited use of military force is to prevent a great calamity. The only good reason for retaining a deterrent, nuclear or otherwise, is that its abolition would be likely to lead to greater probability of armed conflict.

The most likely cause of nuclear war in the world today arises, of course, in the context of East-West relations, and cannot be discussed in isolation from these. There is, it is true, a possibility of a war being started by a minor power which succeeds in manufacturing nuclear weapons. This, in my judgement, is much less serious than the possibility of nuclear war between Russia and the West. Here the whole atmosphere of political relations is crucial, as the case of the shooting down of the South Korean airliner in September 1983 well illustrated. Where there is mutual suspicion and distrust, tragedy can all too easily result.

It will not do to assume too easily, as is sometimes done, that a conventional war between East and West would somehow be a reasonably tolerable state of affairs. One has only to think of the hundreds of thousands killed on a minute area of land by the Somme in 1917, not to speak of the millions killed on the Russian Front in 1939–45, to realize that 'conventional war' is no tolerable option. We have said nothing at all of the various possibilities of chemical and biological warfare which already exist and, indeed, appeared recently in the Iran-Iraq conflict. It has been pointed out, too, that the Jewish holocaust occurred entirely without the use of military weapons. Many more millions have been liquidated in this century in various parts of the world.

I want to return here to what is in many ways *the* central issue of the present time, the possession and the effectiveness of nuclear weapons as a deterrent. The Roman Catholic bishops of North America recently concluded that not only was the use of nuclear weapons sinful, but their possession, with the implied threat to use them if necessary, was also a sin. This does not in itself solve the problem. Often in this life we live in a sinful situation, in which we have to choose between the lesser of two evils. If we abandon the sinful use of nuclear weapons, and the resulting imbalance of military power leads to a full scale war, perhaps with nuclear weapons used on the other side, we may not have fulfilled our Christian duty, but simply been idiots.

The discussion of Christian moral issues has often led to an abandonment of the notions of absolute values

which characterized earlier systems of Christian ethics.
In some ways Christians must regret this change. Yet, as
the writings of Reinhold Niebuhr unforgettably showed,
there are times when a balance of power is required, as
love is worked out in justice. In such circumstances the
understanding of love as an absolute value which
operates in interpersonal relationships may become
unhelpful, due to the complexity of the situation. This
has been a hard and unpalatable lesson for Christian
moralists, but it is most important.

In Britain and elsewhere there has been recent
discussion of the creation of 'nuclear free zones'. In the
Eastern Bloc there have been similar proposals for a
nuclear free Baltic Sea, for example. Yet the people of
Britain might not particularly wish to share in the
present political and social structure of Latvia, Estonia
and Lithuania, even in a nuclear free context. There is
always a balance to be achieved between conflicting
orders of values.

Another sort of nuclear free area is Canada, which
does not have nuclear weapons of its own and hesitates
about such proposals as the testing of American Cruise
missiles on Canadian ranges. Yet many Canadians
undoubtedly consider themselves to be protected against
Russian attack by American nuclear defences. America
could scarcely allow Canada to be invaded by Russia.
This argument is often used in Europe: America could
not allow Western Europe to be absorbed into the
Eastern Bloc, and so we may leave nuclear defence to the
Americans. Whatever the value of this analysis from a
military point of view, to rely explicitly on nuclear
weapons fired by others on our behalf does nothing to
resolve the moral issues involved in the use of nuclear
weapons.

It is pointless to plead complexity as an excuse for
immorality. Yet the complexity of the debate about

nuclear war simply is just built into the problem at every level.[13] CND does an excellent job in making the case against nuclear weapons. It is exploited by Russian propaganda in doing so. This, it may then reply, is a risk that has to be accepted for the sake of the main message.

Most people would agree that disarmament negotiations are to be supported and given urgent priority.[14] How then are they to be conducted? Should one side make 'unilateral' offers and carry them through, in the hope of encouraging the other side and defusing suspicion? In personal relations, such openness is precisely the way to build up trust and to encourage loving relationship. In the complex, impersonal sphere of nuclear arms negotiations the best intentions could lead to the destabilizing of an equilibrium. This might then tempt one side to think that it could win a quick war on the basis of a massive, pre-emptive first strike. This may be an unworthy thought. It is, unfortunately, part of the harsh reality in which we have to live.

Even the question of agreement to limit supplies of weapons is complicated by technical difficulties. If one has to have four nuclear submarines as a minimum number to keep a permanent deterrent patrol operational, then it is pointless to cut this in half. The minimum remains the minimum, if the deterrent is to continue. The whole question of reductions is complicated too by the difficulty of inspection and verification of numbers of weapons, built, tested and destroyed.

Faced with this situation involving a number of unknown factors, I myself would consider a policy of deterrence to be the best option, or at least the minimum evil among a number of greater evils, in the present situation. It must be accompanied by serious and determined attempts at arms reduction negotiations and by the avoidance of provocative gestures by word or action. The whole atmosphere of East-West relations must be improved, if only because we shall quite probably have enormous numbers of nuclear missiles with us till the end of time, whenever that may be.

It does seem to me that a unilateral abolition of nuclear weapons by one side would be more likely to precipitate than to prevent nuclear war, and therefore I regard it as a mistaken policy. However, the problem is far from solved. It may have been justifiable to go to war to destroy Nazism, but it may not have been necessary to burn Dresden or to drop two atomic bombs on Japanese cities. It may be simply wrong, deterrent or not, for Christians to agree to the destruction of the civilian population of the Soviet Union in a nuclear war, even when our own cities are at risk. It ought to be possible to devise a nuclear strategy which will concentrate exclusively on military targets, in order to minimize civilian casualties.

I have not considered the various speculative scenarios involving such phenomena as a nuclear winter, on which the evidence is disputed. It is clear that the risks involved are enormous, and can scarcely be overstated.

Notes

1. There are good surveys of the history of thought and of literature on the subject in RGG 3, *Krieg und Frieden*, and in Hastings Encyclopaedia, War.
2. There is an interesting review of the biblical material from a pacifist point of view in G.H.C. MacGregor's survey, published in the Church and Nation reports of the Church of Scotland. With this one may compare John Baillie's report in the same series for 1944, *God's will in our time*.
3. See Hans von Campenhausen, *Tradition and Life* (1968), 168f., and J.M. Hornus, *It is not Lawful for me to Fight;* cf. too, D.M. MacKinnon, *The Stripping of the Altars* (1968), and R.H. Bainton's superb and readable study, *Christian Attitudes to War and Peace*.

4. K. Barth, Letter to Thurneysen, September 1914, in J. Smart, *Revolutionary Theology in the Making*.

5. Emil Brunner, *The Divine Imperative* (1932), pp. 469ff.

6. Reinhold Niebuhr, 'The concept of order of Creation', in Emil Brunner's social ethic, in *The Theology of Emil Brunner*, ed. Charles Kegley (1961).

7. Karl Barth, C.D. 3.4. 450ff.

8. Paul Lehmann, *Ethics in a Christian context* (1961).

9. Joseph Fletcher, *Situation Ethics* (1966) p. cf. J.A.T. Robinson, *Christian Morals Today* (1964) and Paul Tillich *Systematic Theology III*, 413–4.

10. cf. *Protect and Survive*. HMSO, 1980.

11. Though there are countless books on war there are remarkably few on peace. An exception is J. Hastings, *The Christian Doctrine of Peace* (1922). See too D.M. MacKinnon, *Ethical Problems of Nuclear Warfare, in God, Sex and War* (1963). For a highly critical view of nuclear engineering projects in general see J. Garrison, *From Hiroshima to Harrisburg*, (1980).

12. Commenting on the Church of England's report on *The Church and the Bomb*, Richard Harries suggested that instead of defining moral principles to be applied regardless of the consequences, it might be better to establish moral goals, and then work out policies appropriate to these. It is necessary to consider the theology of power, and the consequences of a unilateral renunciation of nuclear weapons. (*The Times*, 8 Jan. 1983).

13. In debate on this report the Archbishop of Canterbury stated, 'Since I believe that the unilateral approach would undermine disarmament negotiations in progress without exerting much exemplary influence, I cannot accept unilateralism as the best expression of the Christian's moral duty to be a peacemaker.' Basil Mitchell in a letter to *The Times* put it thus. 'What is painfully clear from the debate is that we are faced with an agonizing dilemma which admits of no solution that is free from severe practical or serious moral cost. Neither side escapes it, and if, as I think, the deterrent should for the time being be retained, this policy is tolerable only if accompanied by

the most sustained and determined efforts to find an alternative way of keeping the peace.'

14. cf. the discussion arising from the films *Threads* and *On the Eighth Day* (1984).

4. Personal Relationships: Sex and Moral Values

Respecting persons

Respect for persons has always been recognized as a cardinal principle of Christian ethics, even by those who feel that the principle may operate quite successfully when the original religious context has been discarded. The corollary of loving God is understood in the New Testament to be love of my neighbour. To love one's neighbour as oneself implies treating others with the highest regard. The gospel goes beyond this and suggests that we must learn to love on the pattern of the self-giving love which God himself demonstrated in the life and death of Jesus Christ.

In the tradition the notion of *communio sanctorum* (the communion of saints) has suggested a community of selfless mutual regard stretching unbroken through history into the *eschaton*. In more recent thinking the existential relationship of I-thou encounter, in candid and free communication, has often appeared to suggest an ideal relationship. But this has not been able to function as a norm. For it has also been seen that there are occasions when what is termed as I-it relationship is more appropriate in human relations. If we were to engage in existential encounter with all the people with whom we had daily contact, social life would grind to a halt and society would turn into chaos. Respect for privacy and anonymity, too, are important characteristics of love as much as intensive communication.

It is no accident that the tradition has devoted much energy to discussion of personal relationships in terms of marriage and the family, and sexuality in relationship. These are perennial issues in society, and need to be thought through afresh in swiftly changing cultures. I make no apology for concentrating again on this cluster of themes.

Marriage, according to the confessional record already mentioned, 'is to be between one man and one woman; neither is it lawful for any man to have more than one wife, nor for any woman to have more than one husband at the same time. Marriage was ordained for the mutual help of husband and wife, for the increase of mankind with a legitimate issue, and of the Church with a holy seed, and for the prevention of uncleanness'. We may note the traditional order in Christian thought: the primary category is marriage. Sexuality receives only the negative reference to 'the prevention of uncleanness.'

How are we to speak of these issues and act upon them today? We may not simply repeat the old maxims. Even if we were to wish to maintain the attitudes of our forbears, social attitudes have changed dramatically in Britain, especially since 1945, and so we should be in a highly anomalous position. In his celebrated *Sex in Society* Alex Comfort[1] illustrated the change and the shocked reaction, with two quotations from 1961, one from the superintendent of a remand home and one from a judge. 'Girls we are now getting have no sense of responsibility. They do not know right from wrong and there is only one subject they can talk about, and that is sex. They think it is part of their lives.' 'It is an accepted thing today that these young people seem to attach as much importance to the fact of sexual intercourse as they do to ordering an iced lolly.'

Sigmund Freud has taught us that sexuality enters in the most unconscious ways into very large areas of our personal relationships. His thesis was overdone, but it served at least as a valuable counter to centuries of under-estimation of the power and positive role of sex in society. Michael Keeling has caught the significance of this dimension well. 'Sexuality enters into most of the activities of our daily lives; a man's feelings when driving a car, the aunts and grandmothers clucking over a new baby, the crowd at a football match or the school master training a boy's team, the worshippers in church on a Sunday morning, the crowd at a Billy Graham crusade or the devotees of the Blessed Virgin or the Sacred Heart, two friends who enjoy each other's company, the lover and his lass, or the couple with fifty years of married life together – all these are experiencing an excitement (noticed or unnoticed) which is connected at least in part with the sexual instinct. It is within this general pattern of sexual feelings that there occur the direct and recognizable experiences which we call "love" and "sexual desire".'

It might well be thought that in any of these relationships stress might be more appropriately laid on the category of the personal, or the human as such, rather than the sexual as such. Yet there does appear to be this pattern of sexual feeling within which the conscious phenomenon of sexual desire may or may not arise.

Sex and the new morality

In many Western countries, and with important cultural exceptions, the twentieth century has seen a revolution in attitudes to sex, and indeed to morality in general. This change in attitude is by no means confined to the young. The new morality is not particularly new. In his book, *The New Morality*, published in New York in 1928, Durant Drake stated that 'By the "New Morality" I mean the morality which, basing itself solidly upon observation of the results of conduct, consciously aims to secure the maximum of attainable happiness for mankind'.

If we think of the old morality, we may characterize this as involving a prescriptive theory of ethics, in which certain rules are laid down. This may be described, usually in a pejorative sense, as an absolutist theory of morals. In a Christian context there are some rules and acts, it is held, which are specifically commanded by the Bible and the Church. These are always, and for everybody alike, right. There are other acts which, because they are specifically forbidden by Bible or Church, are always, and for everybody alike, wrong – as in the section on moral theology in Denzinger's *Index Systematicus*. These are the standards which can and must be applied always, everywhere and by everyone. The unchanging element in God's revelation is not some intention or purpose but the content of a particular command. The various laws are relevatory definitions of the nature of love. This has, of course, tremendous advantages. If one abandons these prescriptions, one is left to define for oneself the nature of love. Where laws disappear, the line between freedom and fanaticism may become extremely thin.

There are, however, equal fatal difficulties. Legal systems may become more important than the persons they were originally designed to protect. No set of rules is likely to be sufficiently sensitive to cover the full range of human problems. Fixed standards preclude the freedom to decide. In a theological context, the identification of God's will with some given command of fixed content might be held to make God's living presence superfluous, ignoring too the possibility of future or present communication. We cannot be sure that the tradition has itself always made the correct interpretation of God's revelation in the past. If we cannot respond differently to different situations, morality may take on a purely mechanical character.

It is not difficult to see what this comes to in the matter of human sexuality and the institution of marriage. The institution of monogamous marriage is taken to be the biblical expression of the nature and demands of *agape* in the realm of sexuality. One is presented with a clear cut distinction and unequivocal command: marry, or abstain from all sexual activity.

Obviously there are problems with this solution. It has often been observed that there are no actual biblical prescriptions for monogamy in marriage. Polygamy flourishes in societies in which the position of women is frankly inferior to that of men. It may be suggested that if there are moral and theological sanctions against polygamy and in favour of monogamy, these are best understood in terms of an equality between men and women which is more faithful to a Christian understanding of creation and reconciliation. It is maintained, I think with reason, that traditional theories of natural law fail to deal adequately with questions of personal exploitation within marriage, and of whether any institutional structure can guarantee a relationship of true *agape* between persons. Social and cultural convention may become more important than persons. But in that situation we would probably want to emphasize that marriage, like the sabbath, was made for man, and not vice versa.

John Robinson's *Christian Morals Today* was a good example of the new morality. The thinkers in this group do not regard biblical commands as unambiguously and transparently clear expressions of God's intention. God does not speak to us in propositions. We approach the biblical text with certain definite questions, which themselves help to shape the answers we receive. Persons rather than principles, experienced relationships rather than revealed commands are the starting point. The criterion for ethical conduct and decision is Jesus's call for people to subject everything in their lives to God's unconditional rule of righteous love. Different situations demand different responses. 'Jesus never resolves these choices for us. He is content with the knowledge that if we have the heart of the matter in us, if our eye is single, then love will find the way, its own particular way, in every individual situation.'[2]

This position has a lot to be said for it. God's love is the only unconditional claim laid on us: the idolatry that develops when laws are given ultimate sanctity is avoided. Good and right cannot be prescribed antecedently to every situation. This position would appear to be more consonant with the doctrine of justification by grace alone. New occasions teach new duties, and man is able to act responsibly in Christian freedom.

There are difficulties to be solved here too. Everything appears to be left to the judgement of the individual – the corporate element of the Christian life in community is given little weight. The complexity of alternatives in most morally significant situations leads us to seek guidelines, and these appear not to be available. Different people will make quite different decisions, each expecting, through something like a doctrine of the inner light, to be reflecting God's will for him or her.

Coming back to the field of sexuality, the one obligation of the new approach is to show love. No institutional framework can guarantee the authentic expression of sexuality. What matters is the honest and truthful expression in physical relationships of the degree of personal commitment that they represent. What matters is whether the other person is served or exploited. Though the popular impact of his teaching has lain in the opposite direction, it appears that for Robinson in practice the appropriate conditions are met fully only in marriage. Most theologians would probably agree, though they would want to allow that special circumstances require individual solutions.

Sexuality

The ethics of the new morality is a conscious turning away from the traditions of Catholic moral theology. There are, however, other options. Helmut Thielicke's *Theologische Ethik* is the largest twentieth century Protestant treatment, and the section, *The Ethics of Sex*, is probably the largest modern theological treatment in English. Thielicke believes that there is a 'biblical anthropology of the sexes', involving the traditional Lutheran concept of orders of creation. 'The differentiation of the sexes is so constitutive of humanity that first it appears as a primeval order (Gen.1.27) and then endures as a constant despite its depravation in the Fall. All depends on the proper theological understanding of man. Wherever sexual chaos, i.e. the exchange of partners at will, prevails, we are confronted with a crisis, a breakdown of personal being, or personality.' In sex both *agape* and *eros* are involved. The person to whom I relate myself erotically must be my neighbour, and hence the object of my *agape*, but not everyone who stands in *agape* relationship to me can be the object of my *eros*. What is the nature of the *eros*, *libido* or sex instinct? It is 'the desire, accompanied by pleasure and the urge to consummate this pleasure in ecstasy, for psychophysical union with another human being'. It may be sublimated in mystical love. As a dimension of human existence it is a mystery, protected by a sense of shame.

What then is the precise relationship of sex to marriage? For Thielicke marriage is an order of creation, preceding the fall. In the New Testament the Pauline comparison between Christ and the Church gives it a place also in the order of redemption, with both a worldly and a spiritual side. This dual character was recognized by Luther for whom the spiritual benediction of marriage was for those only who had faith.

In this context Thielicke looked at divorce and the remarriage of divorced persons. Jesus declares in the New Testament that marriage in the sense of God's original order of creation is indissoluble, and describes entrance into a new marriage as adultery (Mark 10.1ff.; Matt. 5.32; Matt. 19.3ff.; Luke 16.18). In the earliest community, only the adultery of the wife, and a mixed marriage in which the pagan partner demands or carries out a divorce, justifies divorce. (I Cor.7.15). For Thielicke, 'The contradiction between the conditional allowance of divorce and the radicalism of the order of creation is only a symptom of the deeper contradiction or tension between this present aeon and the original will of God'.[3] When a marriage breaks down there is guilt on both sides. This guilt has legal aspects, since marriage is a contract in law, but it, also, of course, has theological aspects. Therefore the Church should have a part in divorce if it has a part in the marriage. Can the Church overcome the prohibition against marriage of the New Testament? The words of Jesus and the precepts of the early Church cannot be converted into binding laws. Where there is real repentance, remarriage may take place under the awareness of the forgiveness of sins.

In thinking about war and peace we examined the approach of Emil Brunner. His analysis of marriage follows the same underlying principles! 'Where marriage is based on love' he can say, 'all is lost at the very outset' (p. 344). For love is a fluctuating emotion. Monogamy is an order of creation. After the fall, sex includes an evil element. 'Domestication of the wild erotic element is one of the blessings of marriage. On the other hand, and most significantly, since the law and the gospel are not identical, it is the curse of Christian morality that it always regards the most legalistic view as the most serious.'[4] Laws have exceptions. Here it may be thought that we come very close to situation ethics, but in the most solemn and exalted tones. I shall not take up space in examining Bonhoeffer and Barth on this subject in detail. (For Bonhoeffer see *Ethics*, pp. 173–180, and for Barth *Church Dogmatics*, 3.4.116–240, on 'man and woman'.)

Sex and marriage

In the face of all these various and often dubious guides, how are we to reformulate a Christian view of sexuality and of marriage? Classical Christian faith has always held that God in Christ has identified with all of human nature. Notions that the body is evil or inferior to the spiritual realm were quickly ruled out in principle, though they often lingered on in practice. I would want to begin then from the recognition that the whole human condition is part of God's good creation. Sex should be valued as a gift of God, to be handled appreciatively. People who have children may assist God's purpose in sustaining the universe. But this is not the only function of sex. It has been suggested that without being married and having children it is hardly possible to be a real Christian or even a real man or woman. This is, of course, absurd. But there is a sense in which the Christian maintains that he is not the creator *de novo* of his children; they too are a gift from God.

As part of the gift of creation sex is understood then to be good. In the New Testament Jesus is reported to have blessed marriage and implied that it is ordained by God. Throughout the Bible indeed human sexual relationships are used to illustrate God's attitude towards his creation, sometimes affirming (Hosea and Gomer) and sometimes denying (David and Bathsheba) the relationship which God desires between himself and the created order.

In the Bible then, sex has a twofold function in human life. It is obviously a means for procreation. At the same time it is a way to express and establish community between persons. Sexual love is not a thing but an attitude, an inclination to affection and goodwill. It makes some sense to say that in God's action love precedes creation. Because he loves the world God relates to the world. People fall in love before they have children and the children are regarded as an expression of the love and affection of their parents. On the other hand, there are innumerable occasions on which people quite properly make love without any intention of producing children, occasions in which intercourse is intended as a means to, and enhancement of, community between the two people involved.

There is an important sense in which we do not have sexuality, like pseudo-Aristotelian substance, but we are sexuality. This is one of the ways in which we relate to each other at depth levels of personal experience. Though we have reproductive organs which perform a function for us, what we do with them expresses who we *are* in relationship. From this perspective love, marriage, rape, adultery and fornication take on some human meaning. They signify a certain quality or lack of it in relationship. Here human sexuality is distinguishable from that of animals and plants, in the way that human relationships in general are distinguished, though they may also descend to the same level, as in wars.

Christian norms of sex and marriage are expressions of love. This may not mean that in all cases anything goes as long as two people love each other. The truth of Augustine's 'Love, and do what you like', is qualified by the need to see the whole range of the social dimensions of love. Love is a multidimensional relationship which cannot always be limited to what goes on between two people. To say this is not, of course, an invitation to invade privacy. Rather, the person in love may become aware that God, self, beloved and society are all involved in a given loving relationship.

No merely institutional circumstance can authenticate sexual union. But the range of loving responsibility includes an obligation to God and society. In such a situation in modern society, most people have found that monogamous marriage offers the best means of fulfilling this responsibility. Sexual intercourse can take numerous forms, along a spectrum ranging from rape to union grounded in love, in regard for the well being of each other in the presence of God. In something like the latter form, it expresses a certain quality of relationship between persons. (This is not to say, of course, that the sexual relationship is the only kind of deeply loving relationship, but for many people it will in fact help to express their deepest relationship.) In such cases intercourse is an activity which seeks the well-being of the other as well as the self, seeks to serve rather than exploit the other. It has moral worth to the extent to which it is rooted in mutual respect and affection. Marriage often springs from such a love, and gains its stability not from an institutional character but from the element of fidelity. Here the human possibility of belonging to each other is realized in a special way. Provided that the analogy is not understood in a mechanical fashion, this relationship can be seen to be both derivative from and a paradigm of the Christian's communion with God.

Commitment

People marry for all sorts of reasons, for social, political and economic reasons, under family pressure, as a convenient means of having intercourse without fear of public scandal (an increasingly unnecessary reason, in the days of efficient contraception). People have viewed their husbands and wives in all sorts of ways. Bacon, after all, said that wives are young men's mistresses, companions for middle age and old men's nurses. It is a social institution with legal aspects, involving a contract between a man and a woman, which has a certain binding force in law. It is not, according to the Reformed Churches, a sacrament. It is not even a special means of grace. People who are married are certainly not better off before God than people who are not. It is not, in my view, an order of creation (I'm not sure what that would be in any case). It is not *the* exemplary instance of human relationship in the I-thou dimension, with a special correlate in Christ's relation to his Church. It is indeed a contract, first made by two persons and thereafter perhaps blessed by the Church. But it is a very special contract in that it involves a *total* claim of two persons on each other.

This is a long-standing obligation. Karl Barth said of marriage that 'It consists essentially in the life-partnership established and subsisting between these two, a man and woman' (*Church Dogmatics* 3.4.187). Not every marriage does, in fact, last for life. But unless it is entered into with the intention at least of being continued for life, the sense of claim and mutual obligation is likely to be less than total. This intention, obviously, normally exists since marriage usually springs from love which involves both sexual attraction and mutual respect and affection, regard for the whole personality of the other person. Including in this wider sense the element of fidelity, it is not limited to a given passing moment of sexual attraction. Christians ask in the marriage service for God's grace to help them to continue in living together in love to each other and to God.

There is then, and it is perhaps surprising how this needs to be emphasized, much more to marriage than sex. Luther discovered this quite early, and his references to marriage change from emphasis of the sexual aspects to emphasis on the domestic pleasures of home and companionship. A marriage without sex is an unusual and probably precarious affair. But the tradition deserves full marks for the initial assertion that 'marriage was ordained for the mutual help of husband and wife'. Since marriage is not a sacrament, since nothing happens by magic, 'mutual help of husband and wife' is not something instantly and perpetually realized. Marriages are not necessarily the gateway to instant paradise: they have to be made. Love must learn to be more loving, more sensitive, better informed, more differentiated in action. To this extent marriage is a paradigm of all human relationship and of Christian life in particular: it is easy to speak, but hard to learn to listen.

Divorce

Marriages do in fact break down, despite the best of intentions. It may well be that where divorce is easy and socially perfectly acceptable, people do not always try as hard as they might otherwise do to rebuild relationships that are not irreparable. Since, too, divorce usually involves more than two people, it is not always a service to society to make the obtaining of divorce easy.

Christians understand marriage to be based on love which involves regard for the whole person of the other as a person in the sight of God. If mutual affection breaks down completely, if an irremediable breakdown of the marriage has taken place, and no amount of outside assistance, which of course one has a duty to seek, can resolve the conflict, then out of regard for the other as a person a divorce may be the appropriate solution. A divorce usually involves more than the couple. The damage which will be done in these other areas of responsibility must be weighed against the damage which will be done by husband and wife to each other by remaining married. Even here it may be that the primary duty is to the husband or wife, even the duty of divorce. On the basis that marriage is concerned with the whole person as person, it will be agreed that no single cause, even adultery, should itself be a ground for divorce, unless this itself causes irremediable breakdown. Not all Christians would consider a single instance of adultery unforgivable, though it would certainly give cause for urgent reappraisal. If divorce is on occasion appropriate, then the remarriage of divorced persons may also be appropriate. Remarriage may then take place in church, if the priest or minister conducting the service is satisfied that the remarriage is appropriate. In a tradition in which marriage is not a sacrament, the issues involved for traditions in which marriage is a sacrament are not applicable.

Complexity

I want to consider now a number of further issues related to human sexual relationships, beginning with the question of extra-marital and pre-marital sex. For traditional theological ethics the issue does not really constitute a problem. It is not permitted. For Thielicke, 'there is denied here one of the essential purposes of sexuality, namely a personal relationship designed to be permanent and the willingness to accept the office of parenthood, so here sexuality loses its essential nature'. If, however, one takes a hint from the Reformers and sees the basic role of sexuality in the area of personal relationships as much as in the function of procreation, then the order of discussion may be rather different.

We need not linger very long over the issue of extra-marital sex. If marriage for the Christian involves a total claim, which is at the same time an exclusive claim, for a life partnership, then a sexual relationship with a third person damages the totality of the claim. Sexual relationships after divorce or years of separation are clearly not extra-marital in that sense. The sin of adultery is not so much against the divine ordinance *per se* as against the husband or wife as a person, and *so* is a sin against the God of love.

What then of pre-marital sex? Where this involves exploitation of the other it is, for the Christian, clearly wrong. But we may be thinking of the couple, who have been in love for a long time, and are perhaps engaged and intending to marry. They are willing either to take on the responsibility of parenthood or to use efficient methods of contraception. They may feel that it is only in full sexual union that they can fully express their commitment to each other. Given that there is love and full commitment on either side it would seem that pre-marital intercourse cannot be ruled out *a priori*. On the other hand, the couple may be taking on a responsibility which they may not always be able to bear without the supporting framework of the institution of marriage, for we are not spiritual athletes and paragons of perfection, but more often *simul iusti et peccatores* (justified and sinners at the same time).

We might mention some of these areas of responsibility. It has to be said that there is no completely efficient form of contraception, and that the most efficient, the pill, shows an increasing incidence of risk for the woman who is using it. Love is unlikely to require us to involve those whom we love to take risks on our behalf, however willing they may be to take them. Though practice is said to make perfect, it cannot be automatically assumed that pre-marital sex will be beneficial. Kinsey noted long ago that pre-marital experience sometimes gave rise to feelings of insecurity which upset sex life later in marriage. One cannot be sure of the outcome, yet one is dealing with a human person. Sex for most people is not just an appetite like that for food, but it involves a giving of oneself. Marriage involves a dimension of totality of claim and of continuity which is not always present outside marriage. Even the decision of two people in private that they love each other may not perhaps involve a claim as total as is involved in public acceptance of mutual responsibility in marriage. Engagements can be broken off, and should be when necessary.

It should be said, too, that the needs of a woman in sexual relationship may be rather different from those of a man. Yet the woman is often put in the position of having to show that she is really committed by permitting intercourse. She may even want a baby, but she may not want it to come into a situation of insecurity. Sex may often involve the whole life of a woman more than the life of a man. Christians know that they are not always moral athletes, any more than spiritual athletes. Therefore they should have no illusions about themselves, and perhaps they should take the frailty of their motives at a particular time seriously.

What the Christian will do in such a case will depend on the situation, but not just on the situation, for he or she will wish to act according to the pattern of love shown through Jesus Christ. It is this context of ultimate caring for the other as an individual, and as an individual within the by no means perfect society in which we live, that decisions about pre-marital intercourse should be made.

Homosexual relationships

We now come to another source of endless anxiety and agonizing in the Christian tradition, the area of what is often called sexual deviation. The term is used to indicate difference from the normal, average or usual type of sexual activity in our society at the present time, though of course, all kinds of different norms have obtained and do obtain in different societies at different times. Sexual deviation can cover the widest range of activities. Anthony Storr's list ranges from sado-masochism, fetishism and transvestism to exhibitionism and sodomy of numerous kinds. Most of these problems can be safely left to the psychiatrist, despite the morbid interest in the topic shown by much traditional moral theology. I shall confine myself to those areas involving personal relationships in which a total commitment in love may be made. This is particularly the case in the matter of homosexuality. The tradition has tended to deal here almost exclusively with male homosexuality, but the question of female homosexuality is equally important. Since it has been less generally proscribed by law, the latter has aroused less interest among moralists. Both men and women may be attracted to the same sex. Such attachments, Storr reminds us in his important study, *Sexual Deviation*, are an important part of the process of growing up. All of us, he considers, tend to be fascinated by and to fall in love with people who represent some aspect of ourselves which is not finding expression in actual life. As a girl grows up, says Storr, by being able to identify herself with an adult woman she automatically withdraws the projection which, in earlier years, lent older women a kind of glamour for her. Many girls fail to take this step. Women who are predominantly homosexual usually show evidence of a deep sense of insecurity in general. Many factors of deprivation, often relating to parental background, cause this lack of maturity. Some women believe that their relationship is deeper than would be possible with any man. But, Storr concludes, in fact they do not know what they are missing. For some women a homosexual way of life may be much better and happier than frustrated loneliness, but this is not to say that it can ever be fully satisfying. The point is often made, and should be emphasized, that people with homosexual inclinations often experience a level of loneliness which it is almost impossible for other people to conceive of.

All this applies equally to male homosexuality. The

patterns appear to be similar, and the choice lies between extreme loneliness and relations which, though they may appear to be highly satisfactory, are often highly unstable and are probably never as fully satisfying as relationships with the opposite sex can be. Quite apart from difficulties in the private relationship, such as a frequent rivalry rather than complementarity between the partners, the lack of the social supports of marriage – the very reverse of this, the threat of exposure, blackmail and the like, tends to make the way of life precarious and unsettled. We may not dismiss this issue as simply one for the psychiatrist. If the Christian is called to care ultimately for all his fellow men, his concern must be an informed concern and he should view this human problem in the light of faith.

If we turn to the theological tradition for advice, we find ourselves in a very different atmosphere of evaluation from that of the social worker. There must be few human activities on which divine judgement has been more colourfully predicted than homosexuality. Thielicke quotes the Lutheran theologian Benedict Carpzov as listing as consequences 'earthquakes, famine, pestilence, Saracens, floods, and very fat, voracious field mice'. Karl Barth, for whom the *imago Dei* in man is the distinction between male and female, is scarcely less severe.[5] Yet our concern must be with the concrete reality of the situation of my neighbour.

I would want to sum up an approach to this problem in this way. First, the homosexual person is my neighbour quite as much as the heterosexual person, and therefore requires the same sensitive and sympathetic concern. Homosexual inclination is no more sinful *per se* than heterosexual: all have sinned, and fall short of the glory of God. In so far as is possible, all medical and social help should be offered to the individual concerned. The evidence does appear to show that homosexual relationships, on an individual basis and in society, tend to be much less satisfying than heterosexual. People should be encouraged where possible to the more satisfying. Christ came to give life more abundant, lived not in the shadows but to the full. Where, however, no change of attitude occurs, the Christian's concern should be devoted wholeheartedly towards enabling the homosexual to live as full a life as possible under the only conditions in which he can live. This should happen without reservation or censure, but with the love which should go out to the disadvantaged in society. For it was the lost which the Son of Man came to seek and to save. If we may regard homosexuality as a disability or a handicap, then clearly it is the duty of the Christian, and indeed of every citizen, to encourage and assist the person involved, rather than to accentuate the effects of the handicap.[6]

In conclusion, we ought to remember that there is still much disagreement among the experts about the nature of homosexuality. We have taken the view that the conscience and indeed the self-understanding of gay men and women ought to be respected, and undoubtedly such people ought to be treated with the respect which they both expect and deserve. However, it is sometimes suggested that the gay movements are themselves in some respects a mistaken reaction to an artificial situation. In this perspective, homosexuality as a decisive characteristic of personality is seen as a category invented by psychologists in the nineteenth century, in a new scientific approach to human sexuality. Homosexuality was seen as a negative trait, and gay liberation arose in response, to see the phenomenon as a positive trait instead. It may be simply foolish to characterize the personality of intelligent human beings according to what they do in bed. The position is rather that there have always existed in society individuals who are more orientated towards the same sex than others, and this has been recognized and accepted by many societies in history. With the rise of 'sexology', those who were typecast reacted by expressing an element of their general human sexuality in genital terms in an exclusive manner, thereby creating an unnecessary ideology of homosexuality.

It may be that this will increasingly come to be regarded as an important perspective on this matter. Meanwhile we must respect the views of those who take a positive and even exclusive view of gay culture. If they are mistaken, it is often the rest of society which encourages them to err. The error is often compounded by savage persecution, of which the Nazi extermination of several hundred thousand gay people in concentration camps is justifiably seen as a paradigm case.

It is sometimes held by traditional moralists that homosexual relationships must be especially sinful by definition, because on a Christian understanding sexual relationships are in the first instance given for the procreation of children, and this is excluded here. But as we have seen, Christians have often thought that the mutual help and support of husband and wife is at least as important in Christian understanding as procreation. It may be recognized that intercourse for the sake of sexual pleasure and delight in each other's company alone is entirely proper. This will apply as much to homosexual as to heterosexual couples. There are, however, as we indicated above, better grounds for caution.

Here, as in all areas of personal relationships, respect for and sensitivity to individuals as each a unique child of God is absolutely central.[7]

Notes

1. See Alex Comfort, *Sex in Society*. There are a number of good short studies on the subject; cf. too O. Schwarz, *The Psychology of Sex*; A. Storr, *Sexual Deviation*; K. Walker, *The Physiology of Sex*; R. Hettlinger, *Living with Sex*; M. Keeling, *What is Right?*
2. J.A.T. Robinson, *Christian Morals Today*, 34ff.
3. H. Thielicke, *The Ethics of Sex*, 25ff. cf. Basil Mitchell: 'The Christian "theology of marriage" is concerned primarily with the life-long commitment of one man and one woman to each other' (Law, Morality and Religion, 113).
4. E. Brunner, *The Divine Imperative*, pp. 340–383.
5. K. Barth, *Church Dogmatics*, 3.4.166. Cf. Peter Coleman, *Christian Attitudes to Homosexuality* (1980), and H.A. Williams, *Some Day I'll Find You*, 1982.
6. As David Brown says in his excellent *Choices*, 'A church that attempts to impose its views by force rather than persuasion will inevitably in the end reap a whirlwind.'
7. There are excellent discussions of ethical issues in personal relationships and in medical decisions in the *Journal of Medical Ethics*.

5. Medical Issues: Respect for Life and Respect for Persons

In turning to Christian concern for medical ethics we meet issues which give rise to fierce controversy. Here different Christian groups hold, and are likely to hold, radically different opinions, and no proposals are likely to meet with unanimous agreement. The field of medicine has always been subject to various taboos and rituals, both in primitive and in modern societies. Various religious groups have, for example, refused to allow blood transfusions in recent times. The development of medical science was long subject to the development of theological theory. It might indeed be thought that the history and practice of medicine is largely the history of its emancipation from the mystifying and inhibiting clutches of the theologians. Yet things are not so simple. Medical theory and practice are indebted in important respects to the culture in which they are carried on. On occasion it has been Christian ethics which has given rise to concern and action about pressures on medicine deriving from particular ideologies, notably the forced sterilization of people thought ethnically substandard by the Nazis in Europe in the 1930s.

In chapter two we considered the question of health care. Now we must turn to the specific issue of the preservation of life as such. Medical practice has always been understood as involving action for the benefit of the patient, in terms of the Hippocratic oath. The major religions have been concerned to maintain the sacred

character of life. The Judaeo-Christian tradition is no
exception. 'Thou shalt not kill.' Historically of course the
theology of the just war and retributive theories of justice
have led to widespread exceptions to this rule. But, as
God's creation is understood as good, and life itself as a
gift from God, so respect for life will always be a notion at
the centre of the Christian consciousness. Life is a gift
from God, and it is not up to man to decide when it shall
be continued and when it shall be withheld.

Practical decisions are often hard. What is to be done
when two claims to life conflict, e.g. when the life of an
unborn child may be saved at the cost of the life of its
mother? We are driven to examine the notion of respect
for life more closely. Do we mean something identical
with respect for persons? Do we have some prior
understanding of 'life' as such? When does life constitute
a person? What do we mean by persons?

In the nineteenth century there were fashionable
trends in the so-called philosophy of life, 'Vitalism',
associated among others with the French philosopher
Bergson. We may think too of Albert Schweitzer's
philosophy of 'reverence for life.' The purpose of
Christianity is not necessarily to underwrite fashionable
trends. The same applies with equal force to Aristotle's
understanding of living beings, filtered through the
tradition of medieval scholastic philosophy.

What is life?
What, precisely, is life? When does a living human
organism become a person? When does this organism
then cease to be a person? What is death, and how can it
be measured? Here is a maze of complex questions in
philosophy and in clinical medicine. When does human
life begin? Perhaps the most obvious answer to this
question is to say that it begins when the human female
ovum is fertilized by the human male sperm. There is

created a zygote, an egg with all that is required to produce a fully developed human person, given an appropriate environment in which to develop. This is the time of 'conception'. Here, too, human life often ends, for it is clear that a large percentage of zygotes die before implantation in the mother's womb. For those that survive, within a day or two there is implantation, and the conditions for development are now complete. Is this the point at which we may speak of a potential human person? The early Fathers debated the exact time when a soul was created. Moral theologians later distinguished between the appropriate penance for an artificially induced abortion before and after 'quickening' as felt by the mother. In legal practice, too, the time of quickening was used as the time when it became proper to speak about a person within the view of the law.

It has often been argued, as we have seen, that Christian concern ought in the first instance to be a respect for persons, as sentient beings in relationship with each other and with God, rather than concern for an abstract concept of 'natural life' of a purely physical sort. Some modern thinkers have seen the development of the cerebral cortex, at perhaps about forty days, as a convenient standard of measurement. Yet there are clearly problems with regarding the foetus before that period as simply one of the 'products of pregnancy' as it has been termed.

Sometimes it has been thought that a foetus is not to be regarded as an autonomous person till it is born, and capable of independent survival outside the womb. Yet modern technology has made the period of birth a question of clinical judgement rather than inevitability, and in many ways the infant remains dependent on the mother long after birth. Indeed the advent of *in vitro* fertilization and development makes possible some shortening of the time spent in the womb at the beginning as well as at the end of the process.

Clearly it is difficult to be precise in the matter of when a foetus becomes a person. It is tempting to take refuge in the dicta handed down by Christian moralists in the days before scientific medical knowledge was possible. Often these dicta are valuable as warnings that care must always be exercised. Life is a gift of God, and it is not up to man to take it irresponsibly. Yet difficult practical decisions have to be made. It is in recognition of this hard fact that the Churches have set up working parties on these complex issues in which professional research workers are represented. There are no magic formulas in Christian ethics, any more than there are in other areas of theology. To pretend otherwise is to do no service to God or man.

Something should be said here about *in vitro* fertilization and its further development (*in vitro*, i.e. in a glass, rather than *in vivo*, in a living body). Christian ethics has to reflect on the position with some care. It may be argued with much weight that it is foolish to spend inordinate time and energy setting up committees to discuss an issue which is concerned with the health of a minute fraction of the world's population at a time when a vast number of people die weekly from malnutrition and other diseases associated with poverty. It is clear that a sense of balance and proportion is important in terms of the time and money devoted to different projects. Still, the matter of *in vitro* fertilization raises important issues of principle and of practice.

It has become possible to take eggs from a woman's ovaries, fertilize them in a laboratory with male sperm, keep the fertilized eggs in development for up to a fortnight, and then implant the egg back into the mother's womb. The basic problem is how far it is justifiable to take risks which may produce offspring with physical or mental handicaps, some of which may conceivably not appear till many years after birth. The process of *in vitro* fertilization has been practised for some years on animals with considerable success, and more recently perfect human babies have been born. There is no reason to think that the risks need to be greater than in other areas of medicine. But clearly great care has to be exercised.

Other practical problems arise. It would be possible to develop fertilized eggs to a certain point for research purposes, and then to destroy them, especially if they are defective. How far is it justified to go on growing foetuses where the pregnancy cannot be brought successfully to term in the mother's body. What are the rights of these 'products of pregnancy' who are incipient human beings?

Research and development bring new risks, here as in all medicine. In animals, for example, semen has been frozen and then used successfully after long periods. How far is the risk of damage in processes of production acceptable in the case of human beings?

In vitro fertilization

We are now on the verge of the possibility of all sorts of developments of a kind that give rise to speculation and to charges of irresponsibility. There is talk about producing human beings by a cloning process, of producing children of fathers long since dead, of bringing infants to full term in laboratories, without father or mother in the traditional sense. It is important to retain a sense of proportion. Many of the science fiction scenarios created, often by opponents of any sort of *in vitro* fertilization, are far from possible, both on technical and on economic grounds. Where there is human activity there is always room for irresponsibility. But we are in fact concerned with questions asked by highly responsible research workers.

There is no doubt that in time technical advances will

be possible which are inconceivable today. It must be said that this is one of the 'grey areas' in which it is difficult to lay down hard and fast rules. Yet a general statement is not enough. It is precisely awareness of the dilemmas which drives people to seek more detailed guidelines. Here the Christian understanding of man as in some important sense unique, as made in the image of God, must mean that people cannot be regarded simply in the same light as animals. Special care must be taken so that the lives of incipient human beings are protected. However, the ways in which this may best be done may still have to be left to the clinical decisions of the professional judgement. Theologians can and must state the Christian priorities, but they cannot specify the executive detail of how this should be achieved. The Christian position here is not different in principle from Christian attitudes to politics or law, where the priorities are stressed and the technical machinery left to those who are professionally competent to devise it.

In the case of problems of human fertility, fertilization may be, of course, by the husband in the case of a married couple or by another donor where the husband is infertile. This raises the whole issue of the overcoming of infertility. Traditional ethics would regard AID as adultery. Yet it is far from clear that this is so, since there is no sense of a deliberate betrayal of a relationship of trust and devotion. On the contrary, the search for such assistance may itself be the expression of a loving, trusting relationship. However, we have to remember that all human activity has important and often unexpected psychological dimensions, and so it is doubtless sensible to preserve the anonymity of the donor in such cases. A similar case arises in the provision of the facility of the so-called surrogate mother, who is prepared to carry to term an infant produced from the fertilized egg of another couple. Here the possibilities of psychological strain and economic abuse are so manifest that the very greatest caution is clearly advisable. If the surrogate mother decided that she wanted to keep the baby, for example, the legal complications of deciding parenthood could be considerable.

It is probably the case that in the area of genetic engineering we are dealing not so much with a completely new situation as with a rapid process of development. We need not so much revolutionary ethical adjustments as a careful application of the rules common to all Christian ethical decision making, no more and no less.

The problem of *in vitro* fertilization is a problem of overcoming infertility. In the next section we shall have to consider the artificial prevention of the creation of life, in contraception. All of these issues come within consideration of the family in society. We have seen that the family is itself an institution which Christians wish to strengthen, but for the fulfilment rather than the diminution of the lives of those who make up the family. As society changes and becomes more mobile, as patterns of employment and education, health and medicine, leisure and all other elements of culture develop, so also will family life. In all these areas Christians must seek to be obedient to the Spirit of God, though not to the spirit of this age, a possible future age or indeed a previous age.

The Warnock Report
The whole question of *in vitro* fertilization has of course recently come again to public notice following the publication in July 1984 of the report of the Committee of Inquiry into Human Fertilization and Embryology under the chairmanship of Dame Mary Warnock, DBE, 'The Warnock Report' (HMSO, London, 1984). After thirteen chapters of clear argumentation the report lists sixty-three recommendations for legislation on the sub-

ject. There are three minority reports, and an extensive list of bodies who submitted evidence and opinions to the committee.

In her preface Mary Warnock acknowledged that 'the issues raised reflect fundamental moral, and often religious questions'. The committee tried to provide a reasoned discussion of the issues, and a coherent set of proposals for how public policy, rather than the individual conscience, should respond to developments in the field. Questions about fertilization arouse strong feelings. Regulation requires guidelines. 'There must be *some* barriers that are not to be crossed, *some* limits fixed, beyond which people must not be allowed to go. Nor is such a wish for containment a mere whim or fancy. The very existence of morality depends upon it.'

Chapter one, The General Approach, recalls the birth of the first 'test tube baby' in July 1978 and the discussion which followed it. The second chapter considers the subject of infertility and its treatment in Britain. Reflecting on eligibility for treatment, the inquiry examined the claims of single parents, lesbian and male homosexual groups and concluded that as a 'general rule' children should be born into a two-parent family with both father and mother, Consultants should be left with the right to decide whether to treat a patient, but should have to give reasons if they refuse.

The report discusses all the current 'techniques for the alleviation of infertility' and approves of them, except for the treatment by which the initial stages of the embyro's development take place in another woman before being washed out in a process called lavage and transferred to the eventual mother. The next extension of this, surrogate motherhood, is rejected, and the committee proposes that assisting it should become a criminal offence. Lavage carries medical risks and the chance of an unwanted pregnancy for the egg-donor if the embryo is not washed out. Surrogate motherhood is full of hazards. 'Many unforeseen events may occur between the moment of entering into the surrogacy agreement and the time for handing over the child, and these may alter the whole picture.' If private surrogate agreements are made, it is recommended that these should have no legal status.

In the case of other treatments for infertility such as artificial insemination by a husband (AIH) or by a donor (AID), these should be available in NHS fertility clinics. There should be appropriate safeguards, such as the need for written consent to treatment by both marriage partners, a limit on the quantity of eggs or semen supplied by any one donor (to avoid inadvertent incest by children produced in this way) and complete anonymity for donors and couples requiring their services.

By chapter nine the report gets on to wider uses of the techniques. Couples who are fertile but in danger of transmitting hereditary diseases should have access to semen, egg or embryo donating schemes. Preselection of sex, which plays an important role in the transmission of some diseases, is not yet possible, and bogus 'sex selection kits' should be brought under legal control. Approval is given to the freezing of human genetic material, apart from eggs which are not yet susceptible of safe and reliable storage. Time limits for storage are proposed, and the committee considered that it ought to discourage the use by a widow of her husband's frozen semen to create a child after his death. Such a child should have no rights of succession and inheritance, to avoid tangled legal disputes.

Chapter eleven considers the possible use of human embryos for scientific research. The Committee considered the development of the 'primitive streak', a heaping up of cells at one end of the embryo after about fifteen days, to be the stage at which the embryo begins the journey to full development as a human being. The committee discussed the moral rights of embryos and agreed that they required legal protection. It was agreed, with a dissenting minority, that research on embryos should be permitted up to fourteen days after the embryo's fertilization. The couple responsible for the embryo should be informed and should give their consent.

Looking in chapter twelve at future developments, the committee examined trans-species fertilization, a technique used in medicine to determine the level of fertility of semen by using it to try to fertilize the egg of an animal, usually a hamster. Such tests should continue but should be strictly licensed, and cross-bred embryos should be destroyed at the two-cell stage (usually about two days after fertilization). The use of embryos for testing drugs should be very strictly controlled, since it could lead to the 'manufacture' of embryos on a large scale. The gestation of human embryos in other species is also unacceptable. Though such speculations as virgin births and cloning are not at present possible, guidelines for unethical research should be established. A statutory licensing authority should be created, to supervise this whole area.

Of the minority reports, one argues that surrogacy arrangements might very occasionally be appropriate, one rejects all use of human embryos for experimentation in research, and the other rejects research on human embryos brought into existence for research or as a result of other research.

A careful reading of the report serves to underline the complexity of the issues involved, and the pace at which research opens new options and requires new ethical guidance. It is possible for religious bodies, for example, simply to condemn all experimentation in large areas of medicine on the basis of canonical scriptures, Christian,

Muslim or other. But even if such a fundamentalist approach to scripture is granted, the issues concerning the nature of life in these areas are themselves highly complex. From the perspective of this study of ours, the approach of a careful argumentation based on the widest possible evidence is highly attractive. In my own judgement, the Warnock Report provides an excellent balance which as a Christian theologian concerned for man as God's creature, and as his new creature through Jesus Christ, I can strongly commend. Other Christians will no doubt disagree with the report's conclusions. In all areas Christian opinion differs. Consideration of the problems of human fertility in the light of God's love for mankind leads me to underwrite the report's main findings with admiration and enthusiasm. One must also respect the arguments deployed by the signatories to the minority reports. But on this occasion it seems clear to me that the majority findings represent the more balanced conclusions. Most human activity involves risk, a choosing between risks and dangers, a lack of absolutes. This is part of Christian life 'between the times' and should be accepted. To conjure absolute values out of complex situations may in the end be more dangerous than to recognize contingency for what it is, and to seek God's grace in tracing a way through it.

Birth control

Perhaps the greatest problem facing mankind in the modern world is the problem of mass hunger and starvation on a huge scale, which is related directly to the population explosion in the twentieth century. Apart from the immediate problem of starvation, the huge rise in global population brings with it increase in tension, strife and innumerable forms of social deprivation. In such a situation the problem of birth control becomes a matter of major concern to society. Questions of contraception and abortion are not simply of concern to moral theologians, often in monastic retreats, but are of existential import to hundreds of millions from day to day.

Hugh Montefiore, Bishop of Birmingham, said some years ago that he foresaw the day coming soon when it would be the duty of all Christians to use contraceptives rather than to abstain from using them. Yet the tradition of the Church – the Church of England even into the 1930s – has been heavily opposed to contraception, a position strongly reasserted lately by Pope John Paul II. I myself, as a theologian, have no doubts about the complete propriety of contraception. Once you accept the theology of marriage as primarily for the mutual help of husband and wife, and not primarily to fulfil the divine command to procreate, then in my view you can agree to the use of contraception. The only question remaining is that of finding the method which is aesthetically least disturbing to use and has the least undesirable effects on the person to whom you are related in love. The choice of method would, of course, be a matter of joint decision for the people involved. The world population explosion and the enormous hardships caused by the production of large families with minimal income or none are, in my own view, argument enough, if concern for the well-being of whole persons is the mainspring of Christian ethics. In view of the statistics on illegal abortions and unmarried mothers in modern society, I should be in favour of free distribution of contraceptives to all who wish to use them, with appropriate publicity recommending their use.[1]

Abortion

The question of abortion is, however, far from straight-forward. Dietrich Bonhoeffer, in some ways the most modern of theologians, felt able to dismiss the practice as 'nothing but murder'.[2] It is interesting to look at what he says. 'Marriage involves acknowledgement of the right to life that is to come into being, a right which is not subject to the disposal of the married couple. Destruction of the embryo in the mother's womb is a violation of the right to live which God has bestowed on this nascent life. To raise the question whether or not we are already concerned with a human being or not is merely to confuse the issue. The simple fact is that God certainly intended to create a human being and that this nascent life has been deliberately deprived of his life. And this is nothing but murder.' There is then a right of life to come, and where abortion takes place, this is always contrary to God's intention and is simply murder. If this is the case, then there is no problem, simply a question of hearing God's prohibition. This is also the position of the Roman Catholic Church, reinforced in the strongest terms by Pope John Paul II.

Consideration of specific cases leads one to believe that the issues may not always be quite so clear cut. We may imagine the person with a number of children, some of whom have congenital defects. Another pregnancy occurs, the family have no income, the mother contracts an infectious disease. The result of non-action will possibly be a dangerous miscarriage or another child with severe abnormality. Cases with a number of these complications are very far from infrequent. Is there to be a therapeutic abortion? There are practical issues here of health, finance, family. There are the difficult ethical questions. Is foetal life potential or actual human life, and in either case, what should be done? The actuality of life has been traditionally related to the time when the soul was created, and this has been the subject of much speculation. If we adopt the traditional Catholic position that every unborn child must be regarded as a human person, with all the rights of a human person, from the moment of conception, then abortion is likely to be ruled out.

The problem remains. From the medical point of view, it could be said that the embryo is still a completely dependent, non-viable organism, and that the risk to mother and child is too great to permit the pregnancy to continue. From the legal point of view, let us assume that the risk to mother and child is probably great enough to make the operation legally permissible. What then of the moral and the theological issues?

Crucial to the issue is one's understanding of what constitutes human life, and whether embryonic or even foetal life can be said to be distinctively human. If one sees abortion as the deliberate destruction of an innocent human life, or a human person with all the rights of any other human person, then, with Bonhoeffer and traditional moral theology stressing again the concept of 'the natural', one will see abortion as essentially murder and prohibit it in all circumstances. It is here presupposed that human values and the law of nature are coterminous, and so the correct conduct of life corresponds to nature. Anything which alters or interferes with the course of nature then becomes morally objectionable. But, as for example G.E. Moore put it in his *Principia Ethica*, 'if everything natural is equally good, then certainly ethics, as it is ordinarily understood, disappears; for nothing is more certain, from an ethical point of view, than that some things are bad and others good; the object of ethics is, indeed, in chief part, to give you general rules whereby you may avoid the one and secure the other. What then does "natural" mean in this advice to live naturally, since it obviously cannot apply to everything that is nature?'[3]

How does the lady in our earlier example balance the responsibility to potential life against her responsibility to the rest of her family? Naturalistic ethics would be giving a simplistic answer to a complex issue. What help may be had from the theologians? Thielicke writes that 'it is far from clear that the mother's life is more precious than that of the child'.[4] God's will is to be inferred from the observation of nature. For Bonhoeffer 'the question whether the life of the mother or the life of the child is of greater value can hardly be a matter for human decision'.[5] For Barth on the other hand, 'human life, and therefore the life of the unborn child, is *not* an absolute'.[6] A careful calculation must be made before God. We cannot always know in advance that we have made the right decision, but we must sometimes go ahead, confident of God's forgiving grace.

When does the embryo become a person capable of living in interpersonal relationships? For murder two conditions are usually required, malice and premeditation. The lady in our example may prefer the lives of her family, and perhaps of herself, to the nascent life in her womb. If she decides to terminate the pregnancy, she runs the risk that the pregnancy might have been normal and that the child would have been born in a healthy condition. She would have to decide without knowing the outcome. But it may be that in faith this is a risk that may quite responsibly be taken. In my view this would certainly be the case.

Euthanasia

The issue of the deliberate ending of life brings up, at the other end of the human scale, the question of euthanasia. The world has an increasing population of elderly people. Many suffer from multiple disabilities. Few, perhaps, fear death itself. But very many fear the processes leading up to death. Might it not be desirable, then, for this process to be expedited so as to ensure as swift and as painless a death as possible?

There have, of course, been societies in which the state has decided that certain persons were unfit to live, and in which they were therefore executed, e.g. Nazi Germany. Most civilized people, and all Christian theologians, agree that this is a grave violation of human freedom, and a usurpation of God's sovereign right over life and death which can only be regarded as murder and never justified.

What, however, of the very old and the suffering? Is there a point at which a doctor may put an end to a man's suffering by helping him to die, even if only in the form of mercifully not applying means for the artificial prolongation of his life? It may be that a patient has the right to have this request granted. On the other hand, it is difficult to see how we can be sure that God does not intend this suffering to be some sort of blessing for the sufferer. Can we take on ourselves that decision of life and death which belongs only to God? In most cases it is clearly not for men to do this. Still, even Barth is careful to admit that 'a case is at least conceivable in which a doctor might have to recoil from the artificial prolongation of life no less than from its arbitrary shortening. But it is now not a question of arbitrary euthanasia; it is a question of the respect which may be claimed even by the dying life as such.' On such an interpretation, which is in my view good, respect for persons as a primary category of Christian ethics remains.

In practice it may be difficult to produce a law that will allow any sort of euthanasia while protecting the individual adequately. It is not easy to be certain that a disease will be fatal. Care must be taken, too, to distinguish between the 'agony' of the relatives who may wish for the end to come quickly, and the feeling of the patient, which may well not be the same (a classic case here is portrayed in Tolstoy's *The Death of Ivan Illyich*). To live is the right of the patient, and it is not to be disposed of too soon by the relatives. But 'the respect that may be claimed by the dying life as such' remains important. It has been well said that the good doctor is aware of the distinction between prolonging life and prolonging the act of dying. 'It is well within the ambit of the doctor's conscience to see that the fight is not too hard to be borne.'[7]

Transplant surgery

This is the appropriate place to consider some further important issues in medical ethics. It is only since the First World War that blood transfusions have become common, and there are still religious bodies which resist them as being against the will of God. Recent years have brought the possibility of corneal grafts, of artificial kidneys, of kidney and heart-lung machines, of kidney, liver and heart transplants, and the development of plastic organs. These have raised new issues. When life can be prolonged artificially, who is to be selected and who rejected? When is the decision to be made that further treatment is of no avail? The Hippocratic oath contains the promise 'I will follow that regimen which, according to my ability and judgement, I consider for the benefit of my patients, and will abstain from whatever is deleterious and mischievous.' The International Code of Medical Ethics declares *inter alia* that 'any act or advice which could weaken the physical or mental resistance of a human being may be used only in his interest'. On the legal side Lord Kilbrandon is on record with the comment that 'without consent even a haircut is an outrage'.

What if the patient is said to be dead and an organ is removed for transplant? According to the Human Tissue Act of 1961 'no such removal shall be effected except by a fully registered medical practitioner, who must have satisfied himself by personal examination that life is extinct'. This is where the problem begins. Organs for transplantation must, of course, be removed as soon after death as possible before they begin to deteriorate. But any suspicion that death or consent might have been anticipated would clearly have grave consequences. When should the machine be switched off? The following guidelines were offered by Lord Cohen, former President of the General Medical Council.[8] First, there should be freedom for the patient or his relations to choose when given all the relevant facts. Second, respect for the quality and dignity of human life (though perhaps not for life at all costs) and for all that concerns one's fellow men should be preserved. As a theologian I would be happy with this approach. For theology as I understand it is not concerned so much with 'life' as such as with respect for human beings as persons in the sight of and recipients of the love of God. What of the right of the patient in all this? He has a right to assume that no treatment will be undertaken without his express or implied consent, and that his own personal interest is the first consideration.

Caring for the dying

We must now consider problems of old age, and the care of the terminally ill. Here again Christians are concerned with the understanding of every human being as a child of God, an individual for whom God is ultimately concerned. If it is thought to be ethically justifiable to prevent the creation of life, as in contraception, is it ethically justifiable to prolong life artificially in the treatment of the aged? There are important distinctions to be made between artificially prolonging life and prematurely ending life. It is clear that the latter is highly undesirable. There is nothing to be said for prolonging needlessly the act of dying. On the other hand, easing the suffering of the patient can be open to abuse. Quite apart from other considerations, public confidence in the medical profession would be seriously undermined if people faced a situation in which, when they were weak and ill, they were unsure whether the purpose of the medication offered to them would be to preserve or to end their lives. And most human activities can be and sometimes are abused for commercial gain. What is required is usually a balance between adequate safeguards against abuse and a caution which prohibits the exercise of enlightened practice because of the possibility of abuse in a tiny percentage of cases.

One of the most valuable recent studies of the rights and responsibilities involved in the care of the terminally ill is contained in the 1983 report of an American presidential commission on the subject. (cf. *The Times*, 22 March 1983). The commission concluded that 'a competent patient's decisions regarding medical treatment should almost always be honoured, even when they lead to earlier death.' Even when various forms of life support have been rejected, patients must continue to receive all the medical care necessary to preserve their dignity and to minimize their suffering. The report stresses the importance of establishing workable decision-making procedures which produce good decisions, decisions which respect the wishes of the patients and support the best interest of those who cannot speak for themselves. The aim of the study is to help dying people – and eventually that includes us all – to face death in our own ways, freed from the unwarranted constraints imposed by confusion or unjustified assumptions.'

The nature of death

We have discussed the nature of life. We must consider also the nature of death, and how it may be defined. This is not just a matter of academic speculation: it has important practical aspects.

Until quite recently the problem appeared not to be too difficult. When the heart and breathing stopped, the patient was dead. In recent years, however, it has become possible to revive patients whose heart or breathing have stopped. If they have not suffered more than a few minutes' oxygen deprivation they may be able to resume a normal life. However, if there was a long period of oxygen deprivation then heart action might be restarted and breathing maintained by a respirator, but important brain cells would be destroyed. In this case, the patient would be unable to maintain either of these functions on his own.

Brain cell destruction can be further divided. Some patients who suffer severe brain damage are in a constant vegetative state. Many never recover any sort of mental function, some very occasionally recover consciousness. Even those who have had severe damage to the higher brain centres continue to have functions of and circulation to the brain.

The other patients have no flow to the brain, and reveal no evidence of brain functions. They are incapable of spontaneous respiration, and are 'brain-dead'. They are entirely dependent on mechanical respiration. Heart beat can continue indefinitely, though it usually ceases after a few days. It is not unusual for brain-dead children to be maintained in this way for a month or more.

When is the individual dead? This becomes a particularly acute problem in the case of possible donors of transplants. Organs of brain dead individuals can be kept 'fresh' for transplant purposes. But in order to use the organs, the individual has to be dead. When is the individual dead? Is it proper to ventilate the body to preserve the organs? We shall have to return to the subject of transplantation and the issues it raises.

The definition of death has recently been the subject of careful investigation in the USA by the President's Commission for the Study of Ethical Problems in Medicine. Death is established, they concluded, when all functions of the brain including the brain stem have permanently and irreversibly ceased. It then proposed a Uniform Determination of Death Act (UDDA) to cope with the problem of diversity of definition in the various American states. 'An individual who has sustained either (1) irreversible cessation of circulatory and respiratory functions, or (2) irreversible cessation of all functions of the entire brain, including brain stem. A determination of death must be made in accordance with accepted medical standards.'

By 1983 this standard had been adopted by twenty-six states and by most of the appropriate professional learned bodies, and this trend appears likely to continue. Nevertheless, there has been opposition. Some have suggested that complete destruction of the brain, not just cessation of function, is required for death. There has been the suggestion that legislation is dangerous, a step on the road to euthanasia. Nevertheless, the most expert consensus, represented typically by the document 'The guidelines for the determination of death' (*Journal of the American Medical Association*, 3 November 1981) endorses the UDDA formulation.

It is clear that the maintenance of brain-dead people on respirators for long periods, because the doctors are afraid to turn off the apparatus through fear of litigation, is highly undesirable, leading to great distress among the relatives. Such situations can be reinforced by the appeal to a supposed religious ground. But there can be no valid Christian objection to the UDDA definition and its implications for patient care. Christian ethics is concerned with the person as a human being before God, created by God to live and die with dignity and to be treated responsibly. Within such a framework it is important that accurate criteria for the theory and practice of the treatment of the dead should be developed.

One of the areas in which adequate definition of death

is crucial is of course in the field of organ transplantation. It is essential that transplant organs are removed while they are in perfect condition, and yet is equally essential that the patient should be dead before such removal is effected. Controversy and litigation has arisen in cases where organs have been removed from brain-dead patients. If doctors are deterred from pronouncing patients dead in time for the organs to be used, clearly the lack of donors becomes an acute problem.

Transplant surgery is again a very modern development, though people had thought of it in the middle ages, and attempts at blood transfusions using the blood of animals were made in the seventeenth century, often with fatal results. (There are religious groups which still prohibit blood transfusions.) In recent years transplant surgery has provided an increase in life expectancy for many people. Against the programmes have to be weighed the costs, perhaps depriving other areas of medicine of resources. Again, in some cases the failure rate has been extremely high. But remarkable progress has been achieved, especially by the use of drugs to prevent rejection of the donor organs (notably in the use of Cyclosporin by Professor Roy Calne in Cambridge).[9]

Animal welfare

Research in transplantation has inevitably involved experiments on animals, before the techniques were used on people. This has given rise to powerful opposition. It can be argued that human beings have no right to exploit animals for their own purposes. Yet granting the strength of this argument, it seems clear that when faced with the choice of preserving human life or animal life, human beings will inevitably choose human life. Christians believe that they are called to be stewards of nature, yet that man has a special place and responsibility within the natural order. It must be said that attempts to attack transplant surgeons by violent means in the name of animal rights cannot be too strongly or widely condemned. At the same time, there is clearly much to be said for legislation to control unnecessary suffering in animals, by rigidly supervising and limiting permitted pain levels, and by forbidding the use of animals for frivolous purposes. These might include some aspects of experiments in the cosmetics industry.

While it is not absolutely clear what it means to say that animals have 'rights', clearly the conservation of wildlife is an important aspect of the stewardship of nature. Much more support should be given by the churches to measures against illegal whaling, the sale of furs and ivory, and similar operations.

Finally it should be said that all attempts to persuade more people to carry donor cards, so that their organs may be used after their deaths for the benefit of others, should be actively encouraged. I should be in favour of an opting out system, which assures consent unless it is explicitly refused.

In all these issues it is clear that a view of persons as human beings recreated in the image of God in Christ is central. We are emphatically not concerned with a primitive ritualistic worship of the life force, and we cannot apply the traditional categories of moral theology to the complexity of modern medicine with an unthinking conceptual fundamentalism. Perhaps nowhere else does the truth of Butterfield's dictum hold more clearly than here. Hold to Christ, and for the rest be uncommitted.

Notes

1. Contraception: education is crucial here.
2. D. Bonhoeffer, *Ethics*, 175–6.

3. G.E. Moore, *Principia Ethica*, 41–2.
4. H. Thielicke, op.cit.245.
5. D. Bonhoeffer, op.cit.176.
6. K. Barth, op.cit.3.4.416f., esp. 420.
7. L. Banks in the symposium *Making Moral Decisions*, ed. D.M. MacKinnon (1969).
8. L.Banks, op.cit.
9. On transplant surgery cf. especially R.Y. Calne in *Journal of Medical Ethics*. I.

6. Respect for Life: Further Issues

The case of homicide
We have been thinking about the medical dimensions of problems of life and death. I want to look now at some other areas of the choice between life and death. What are we to say of the man who kills another in self-defence? Is this theologically legitimate or not? What has Christian faith to say in these circumstances? This problem arose in our consideration of war and peace, and of course, comes up most sharply in nuclear strategies based on so-called first strike capability. Even if self-defence may be legally permitted, it appears a flagrant contradiction of the command 'Thou shalt not kill'. 'You have heard that it has been said "an eye for an eye and a tooth for a tooth": but I say to you, that you do not resist evil but if someone strikes you on the right cheek, turn to him the other too.' So says Jesus in the sermon on the mount (Matt. 5.38–42). Do I really prevent the danger to my own life by killing the aggressor? What am I doing when I kill the other, as though his life belonged to me? Those who seek to defend their own possessions, to be righteous by themselves, shall not enter the kingdom of God. Barth seems to be on the right lines here in seeing the possibility of self-defence as something which is not to be undertaken as a matter of course but only as an exceptional responsibility. Only in an extreme case, and not simply in a mood of self-assertion, can a self-defence which may

include the taking of another's life become possible.[1]
Should not the victim of attack, even though he may do
everything else that is possible, regard the actual killing
of his assailant as forbidden? What if *only* the killing of his
assailant will prevent one's own death? That, in my view,
is an issue the answers to which cannot be given by any
man for his neighbour. For the right to life and the
privilege of laying it down is not at the disposal of a third
party, but belongs only to a man and his God.

Capital punishment

Here we come up against the question of capital
punishment. We might until recently have been disposed
to regard this as a dead letter. But it keeps coming up for
more debate in Britain, and is still very frequently
practised outside Europe. In many societies it has, of
course, been the custom for capital punishment to absorb
and transform the act of self-defence and revenge
formerly undertaken by the individual and his family. In
the interests of general peace, and of equity in individual
cases, retribution was decided by society, which
embraced individuals and families, by the authority and
power of its magistrates and officers. This retribution
often includes capital punishment, for example, in the
Old Testament period and in much of the history of
'Christendom', Catholic and Protestant alike. Looking at
the history Karl Barth asks himself, 'Is it not remarkable
that where its abolition has been carried, it has always
been in the face of a more or less powerful Christian
opposition?' He then goes on to take the abolitionist side
(*Church Dogmatics*, 3.4.437ff).

In medieval Europe and in much of the modern world,
capital punishment presents no great problem. Sentence
is justly pronounced by the state. A member of the lower
classes, with whom we have no personal or social
connection, does the actual job. The idea that we think

responsibly only if we realize and accept the fact that it is we ourselves who do the job in the person of the hangman has not been popular, for obvious psychological reasons. What grounds could we have for killing people?

The usual grounds for such punishment are, first, to protect society by the force of a dreadful example – the deterrence theory. The second favourite ground is to mete out the retribution which the criminal's offence demands. In this theory punishment is often seen as a representation and proclamation in human and earthly terms of the retributive justice of God. Thirdly, punishment is intended to incite the criminal to mend his ways. In the case of capital punishment the third ground is clearly ruled out. There can be no reformation: life is destroyed. Yet what right, it may be asked, has society to let one of its members perish, to declare itself totally incapable of having any further contact with him? What then of the second reason, retribution, in a theological context as the carrying out of divine retribution? Can we identify here the thought of God with the opinions of his creatures? It might in any case be thought that all expiation for human transgression has already been made. As Barth puts it – I find Barth on many ethical issues surprisingly illuminating – 'Now that Jesus Christ has been nailed to the cross, for the sins of the world, how can we still use the thought of expiation to establish the death penalty?' (*Church Dogmatics*, 3.4.443) We are left with the first and simplest reason for capital punishment, as a deterrent, to protect society. It may be thought, however, that when society puts to death one of its members it is involved in self-contradiction. Can we maintain human life by destroying human beings? In any case, as a matter of fact the deterrent does not appear to work. In any normal situation then it would appear that for the Christian view of ethics, capital punishment is ruled out.

What about dictators?

We are not talking about normal situations, it might be said. The modern world includes some very nasty circumstances. Might there not arise situations in which it might be necessary to kill someone for the benefit of mankind in general? This was a real issue in the minds of Bonhoeffer and his fellow plotters of 20 July 1944. Luther wrote a short pamphlet on the topic, the title of which was 'When the coachman is drunk', and it was the subject of many repetitions during the war. The Norwegian bishop Einar Berggrav preached a famous sermon on the topic, which earned him imprisonment for the length of the Nazi occupation of his country. Bonhoeffer put it this way: 'When a madman is tearing through the streets in a car, I as a pastor who happens to be on the scene must do more than simply console or bury those who have been run over. I must jump in front of the car and stop it.'[2] It might be thought, apropos the good Samaritan parable, that the task today would include not just tending the casualties but cleaning up the area so that there would be no more robbers in future.

The Calvinist tradition has always had few scruples about laying low the proud and idolatrous prince in the name of God and Church. There might then be an extreme circumstance, fraught with risk, when there is no way of releasing millions from a tyrannous regime except by killing the tyrant. The exception would not be the rule, and would not arise in the case of capital punishment for murder. There might also be here an extreme justification for war. But as we saw in the case of war, the modern situation has introduced so many complications that no simple formula will cover the issue. The duty of the Christian in the responsible society is to direct his or her thoughts to the concrete preservation of peace now rather than to dwell on the possibilities of participating in war when it comes. By then it is too late, and no amount of reflection will compensate for neglect of the task of maintaining peace in the first place.

We shall go on to consider the political aspects of the life of the Christian in the responsible society. I hope that what has been said of persons in relation, and of medical and legal issues in relation to life and death, has at the same time gone to substantiate the thesis that Christian life, even in its apparently most intimate and personal aspects, always retains the dimension of social responsibility. In important respects humanity is sustained and constituted by the exercise of co-humanity, in response to God who is not alone, but is person in relation, Father, Son and Holy Spirit.

Suicide

There are few things more tragic and more deeply disruptive of family life in modern society than suicide. On the face of it, this is an issue on which the mind of the Church has changed dramatically over the last hundred years or so. As recently as 1823 a London suicide was buried at a crossroads in Chelsea with a stake driven through his body. Right up to 1961, survivors of a suicidal attempt were liable to criminal prosecution. Today the emphasis is not so much on condemnation of one of the deadliest of sins as on the action of a loving, caring community in preventing suicide and dealing sympathetically with the problem. Yet it is not clear that the Churches can take responsibility for promoting an atmosphere in society in which suicide is encouraged. The grim events in South America some years ago in which the followers of the Revd Jim Jones were encouraged to commit suicide, forcing children to die willingly or unwillingly, in the name of an alleged private divine revelation, provide a chilling reminder that tolerance of all possible perspectives is by no means a necessary implication of the love of God for all mankind.

There is a need for revolution in many areas of the traditional Christian official teaching. Yet it is important to be aware of the main outlines of the tradition, in order to use the past as a creative instrument in rethinking the future. St Thomas Aquinas sets out the traditional teaching on suicide clearly in the second section of his *Summa Theologiae* (ST 2.2.q.64, art.5). First he cites arguments in favour of permitting suicide, beginning with the suggestion that suicide does no outside person harm, and therefore is not a sin. He replies with a citation, as often, from Augustine in *The City of God* (1.20). Augustine says, 'we must now seek to understand the meaning of the phrase "Thou shalt not kill". That means, you will kill neither anyone else, nor yourself. For he who kills himself does nothing less than kill a man.' And so, of course, suicide is forbidden. Thomas then goes on to give three reasons of his own why suicide is out.

Suicide is forbidden, first, because every being naturally loves itself. Every being naturally preserves itself in being and resists as far as possible what seeks to destroy it. Whoever kills himself acts contrary to his natural inclination and contrary to love (*caritas*) through which everyone ought to love himself. Taking one's own life is always mortal sin, since it happens contrary to natural law and contrary to love.

Because every part is part of the whole, a man is part of the community. What he is belongs to the community, and so in killing himself a man injures the community (here Thomas quotes Aristotle's *Nicomachean Ethics*, 1115a,26). Thirdly, suicide is forbidden, since life is an endowment given by God to men, and belongs to the power of God who kills and makes to live. The man who deprives himself of life sins against God, just as the man who kills someone else's servant sins against the servant's lord, and just as a sin is committed by the man who takes it upon himself to give judgement in a case outside his jurisdiction. Judgement over death belongs to God alone, as it is written in Deuteronomy 32.39 – 'I kill and I make alive.'

Man's life belongs to God, and so he should take care of it. Nevertheless, as Karl Barth reminds us (*Church Dogmatics*. 3.4.400f) temporal life is not the highest of all goods. A man may be ordered by God to risk it, as Jesus did in going up to Jerusalem. He can understand the absolute prohibition of moral theology. From this, said Barth, there ought not to follow an absolute condemnation, with subsequent ecclesiastical and civil discrimination against the suicide. How can we be sure that every case of self-destruction is really an act of self-murder? We don't know what finally takes place between God and the suicide, and therefore we are in no position to judge. No sin is unforgivable, because God looks at a man's whole life, and not just his last act. 'Bonhoeffer is right,' says Barth. 'One can remain alive out of base motives and end life out of noble.' The truth is not that we must live but that we may. Because of Jesus Christ, no one need be so ashamed of any sin against God or man that he needs to commit suicide. Who can say that it is absolutely impossible for the gracious God to help a man in affliction by telling him to take this way out? What if, for example, a man wonders if he should kill himself rather than betray his friends under torture? But this is the rare exception to the rule. Here Barth has moved a long way from the tradition, in the name of Christ.

I want to pursue this line further. Suicide is indeed a specifically human phenomenon, and needs to be seen close up in psychiatric and sociological perspective like all other human phenomena, rather than pronounced upon with the aid of Aristotle's ethics (Stengel).[3] In recent years more than 5,000 people have died through suicide in Britain annually and nearly 20,000 in the USA. Suicidal attempts have been estimated to be six or eight times as numerous as suicides. Suicide occurs in all periods in history. Death is not the aim of every suicide attempt, which may be a cry for help. Suicide rates tend to understate heavily the truth, since juries are reluctant to bring in verdicts of suicide, especially in Catholic countries. Most people who kill themselves are elderly, and many are physically ill, many are socially isolated, especially in urban communities. The rate is highest among the professional and managerial classes, and among students. Spring and early summer are peak periods. Social factors involving personal relationships are the apparent main cause. In primitive societies suicide is considered evil. In 1946–55, according to Erwin Stengel, 5,794 people were charged with attempted suicide in England and Wales, and of these 308 were sent to prison, the rest being fined or put on probation.

Attempted suicide is at a peak between the ages of 24 and 44; for suicide the peak age is between 45 and 64. Hospitalization, and various forms of social service, may often prevent a later successful attempt. Suicide attempts have the effect of an appeal for help, even though no such appeal may have been consciously intended. Some attempts appear to be a kind of gamble with life.

How can suicide rates be reduced? Prevention of social isolation and integration of the individual with a group appears to be essential. First, however, the isolated individual must be contacted. Here the telephone Samaritans do a most valuable job. Beyond this professional medical help is required. Erwin Stengel stressed the importance of the development of a therapeutic community, not just in hospitals but in society at large. To do this society would have to evolve a new approach to social responsibility and a new social morality. The fostering of such a development would be an important part of the task of what it is to be the Church in the world.

The caring community

What then are we to say about the Christian attitude to suicide? I offer here a few summary observations. (1) Suicide, as the voluntary and considered violent annihilation of one's own life, has been judged differently in different cultures, mainly negatively in primitive cultures and in the Church, but was praised, if done for noble reasons, by the Greeks and Romans. (2) It is very difficult indeed for a philosophical ethic to deny a man the right to suicide. One can even go as far as David Hume and suggest that we should reckon the freedom to take our life as a good gift of God, like the rest of his gifts. Motives for suicide are not always bad.[4]

The Christian general rejection of suicide comes from the gospel. The freedom to live, not to have to live, is a gift of the new creation in Jesus Christ. As Kierkegaard put it, 'he who has faith receives the constant sure antidote to despair, possibility.' There is, however, no reason to think that suicide is unforgivable, any more than any other sin. This awareness has practical consequences for our attitude to the suicide and his family. There may even be a time when a man may obey God in dying by his own hand to save his fellows; this we may perhaps see as self-sacrifice rather than suicide.

Finally, it is clear that the Christian community should itself be a therapeutic community as the body of Christ, the community of reconciliation.[5] This applies to congregations, and to individuals in society, in relation to families, friends and associates in every sphere. Christians in society, if they are to be aware in any sense of the metaphor of being the salt of the earth, are under obligation to work constantly in a therapeutic capacity.

Notes

1. K. Barth, *Church Dogmatics*, 3.4.430ff.
2. Bonhoeffer, *Ethics* (the coachman example).
3. See E. Stengel, *Suicide*; John Hinton, *Dying*. Jessica Mitford's *The American Way of Death* is worth reading.
4. On the question of hanging cf. Cynthia and Arthur Koestler, *Stranger on the Square*, and on the Koestlers' suicide cf. *The Times* for 31 March 1983.
5. The debate about the euthanasia society, EXIT, has focused attention again on suicide. Clearly, if the means for suicide are ready to hand, the depressed may be tempted to use them. The incidence of suicide fell dramatically when carbon monoxide was removed from domestic gas.

7. Justice, Hunger, and the Love of God

World hunger

In the introduction to this book we stressed the importance of the creation of a responsible society. Discussion of the many urgent ethical problems in the succeeding pages, may appear to have shown the complete failure of such attempts. A striking example of world failure to provide a just and fair society, in which God's providential care is seen to be everywhere equally realized, is in the immense problem of world hunger and starvation. Before the problem of hunger many of the ethical issues which occupy moralists pale into insignificance. Even the possibility of devastation caused by nuclear war is arguably of scarcely greater significance than the actual devastation and loss of life which takes place steadily year after year, causing untold misery and tragedy. Since most of this suffering occurs in underdeveloped parts of the world among inarticulate and deprived peoples, it often goes relatively unnoticed. Yet the annual destruction would be the equivalent of the annihilation of several major European or American cities.

Theology and revolution

In the face of such a crushing failure on the part of the 'responsible society' Christians have often turned to the 'theology of revolution' or 'liberation theology', notably in Latin America. In Europe, too, the need for a fresh start has been felt. Jürgen Moltmann has put it this way: 'The resurrection transforms faith from a deliverance from the world into an initiative which changes the world.'[1] This is a serious approach to the problems of Christian social ethics. I want to look first at a single example from the work of a pioneer in the field in North America, Richard Shaull.[2] I am in some respects critical of this approach, but I think that it points to lessons to be learned in social ethics.

Shaull's argument went like this. The development and application of technology has brought in its train a process of rapid social change. In this change all orders in society are losing their sacral character and are now open to the future, to be shaped as man wills. This includes the process of secularization. 'Entire races and classes of people have discovered that their suffering is not inevitable and have thus been awakened to a new hope for a better life. But this hope has not been fulfilled.' Institutional structures for a stable society have failed to adjust to a new order and so are in crisis. It would seem that social revolution is the primary fact with which our generation will have to come to terms. What is to be done? For Shaull, if we hope to preserve important elements of our heritage and contribute to the shaping of the future, we cannot remain outside the revolutionary struggle. Revolution is ambiguous. It represents a passion for the liberation of the oppressed, but it also produces destruction and leads to new injustices.

Revolution on this argument is justified from the biblical narrative. Since God is the creator and ruler of all spheres of nature and society, all social orders, these are temporal realities existing to serve God's purpose for man. They can and must be used and changed in line with this purpose. This is consonant with the strong eschatological emphasis of the Bible, which stresses the dynamic nature of God and the fact that his action moves towards a goal. This is the messianic promise. God breaks down the power of the oppressor in order to establish his justice. 'As the influence of Christ grows, old stabilities are swept away, and the struggle for humanization moves to new frontiers.' Looking for support in the tradition Shaull inevitably found it, in St Augustine's *City of God*, in the struggle for the establishment of the heavenly city within the conflicts of the *civitas terrena*.

But Christians cannot speak now to the revolution by means of treatises in systematic theology. What is called for is 'the presence on the frontiers of revolution of communities dynamically involved in the struggle for humanization and engaged in constant running conversation with their biblical and theological heritage'. The suggestion appears to be of pistol in one hand and biblical commentary in the other.

The dynamics of the revolutionary process are detailed. Those who stand between the lines will be ignored (one might have thought they were more likely to get shot). A Christian perspective should enable revolution to develop a type of institution in which self-criticism and sensitivity to dissatisfaction are built into its basic structures. The kingdom of God always stands over against every social and political order. But each new experience of community points towards the kingdom, towards which we are moving but in which, even now, we participate in a partial way. (This is splendid in the right sort of community, but of course there may be an evil sort of community spirit, as in Nazism, we might reflect.) Thought and action must be orientated towards the future. Has Christianity anything to say about the new structures of a new society? There are three contributions: the fact of forgiveness, which sets us free to act for our neighbours; the awareness of sin, of the ambiguity of all our action; the concept of reconciliation.

Revolutions

What are we to make of the theology of revolution, in this and related positions? There are many things in the above analysis which seem to me to be plain misguided. Much play is made in this and similar approaches with the tradition of political critique and the political messianism of Israelite expectation. It is, however, pretty clear that Jesus himself radically revises the whole ideal of political messiahship, interpreting the messiah in terms of the son of man. To suggest, too, that God reveals himself in his most dynamic way in revolutions is no better than the old gambit that God reveals himself in wars. Interpretation of history and ethical value judgements should not be confused. The will of God is not to be read out of historical events and party programmes.

The concept of revolution we have been considering seems not to be that of the French or October revolutions, which were seen by their authors as once for all events, but rather that of the Maoist concept of permanent revolution. This is fair enough in one sense – *ecclesia semper reformanda*, and the like. But the uncritical use of such concepts so as to suggest that what is can never be right, to suggest that all institutions are in themselves against the will of God, is to be subject to the compulsion of the system with a vengeance; one authoritarian pattern of thought is replaced by another. Shaull, despite his qualifications, often appears to identify ideology and theology of revolution. To borrow some of Bonhoeffer's language, this appears to identify the penultimate with the ultimate, in a manner curiously similar to that of the older American Calvinist benediction of the capitalist society to which it is theoretically opposed.

Having said this, it would be blind to underestimate the very real nature of this contribution to the contemporary ethical debate.[3] Theology has often tended to be wise after the event, and then to bless the squire and his relations. If there can be no general 'theology of revolution' and I find the concept too ambiguous to be helpful, there must be a considered theological response to the situation of the revolutionary. He or she is likely to be an increasingly familiar figure on the contemporary scene, and God, it need hardly be said, is concerned in loving commitment for *all* mankind.

Nothing is easier than for churchmen to make liberal statements about freedom and politics, only to have them torn to shreds with wit and logic by other churchmen engaged in defence of conservative reaction.[4] However misguided much theology of revolution (or of liberation, as it is often called) may be, there are clearly situations, and I think especially of the situation of black people in South Africa, in which appeals to restraint, reason and moderation are encouraged by the oppressor precisely because they can be countered with a show of civility in return, while on the plane of harsh reality nothing changes. In such a situation revolution, in due time, may be necessary. Silence suggests acquiescence and courts failure: hence it was possible for the Nazis to murder millions of Jews and others, even after the facts were generally known outside Germany. It is notable that the Catholic Church, which with some shining exceptions, had such a miserable record in relation to Nazism, has gone a long way towards constructive theological response to oppression and revolution in the third world.

Theology of liberation

'God is in his essential nature love, love characterized precisely and uniquely in the self-giving of God to mankind in the events surrounding the life, death and resurrection of Jesus Christ' (G. Newlands, *Theology of the Love of God*, London 1980, 9). In so far as the theology of revolution or liberation is committed to the implication of that love for the poor and the dispossessed in this world, then I must without qualification support it. Twenty years of writing suggest that this is indeed where its heart lies, in basic Christian commitment. 'Universal love comes down from the level of abstractions and becomes concrete and effective by becoming incarnate in the struggle for the liberation of the oppressed. It is a question of loving all people, not in some vague, general way, but rather in the exploited person, in the concrete person who is struggling to live humanly' (G. Gutierrez, *A Theology of Liberation*, London 1974, 276). This is no place to discuss extensively the respective effectiveness of events and ideas in history, or of traditions of Christian ideas and Christian action. Some events need to be seen and appreciated in order to be effective, at least before man. Other events, like leaving the bath running with the plug in – or starving the hungry – bring automatic results. Some ideas are just fascinating to entertain: others, like the Christian concept of love, include a built-in prescription for specific application. It may be that classical Christian theology has implicitly included all that LT (liberation theology) underlines. Christian love always needs to be spelled out in relation to personal existence and social justice.

On the other hand, and there always is another hand for we are sinners, when the gospel becomes too closely identified with a particular political party or sectional interest something has gone badly wrong. God's grace is for *all* mankind. Rich people may be weary and heavy laden, crushed by personal tragedy. Poor people may engage in merciless mutual extermination. In all cases Christians will pray for grace to be the instruments of God's love, without embarrassment and without sentimentality. Perfect love casts out fear. There is always a case for conservatism in theology, if only because through new ideas experiment proceeds by trial and error, and in the first few years often gets things out of proportion.

It follows that what is needed is critical, self-critical reflection on liberation. Critical reflection is necessary not in order to produce compromises but to be effective. No observer of recent wars need doubt the value of slogans to produce results. But we are concerned with the way, the truth and the life, with the relations between act and being. Here LT must include both critical theoretical reflection and highly specific application to the detail of praxis. As Hegel knew, God alone can alter the whole: it is up to men and women to attend carefully to the details.

Such a critical theology of liberation should not presumably be a sphere of private or sectional intellectual entertainment. The inseparable bonds between meaning, use and truth entail that the underlying concern is the appropriation of God's salvation by all mankind. LT may cast valuable light on deficiencies in the classical theologies of the past, especially where these have been assimilated too closely to particular social and cultural backgrounds. If it is to 'come of age', LT has to take on and contribute to the intellectual and social responsibilities of the whole Christian tradition. This emergence of catholicity is already taking place.

What we call ourselves in one sense hardly matters. He (or she) that doeth the will shall know of the doctrine. Some designations are of course bound to be counterproductive. I would not expect too much help from a theological National Front. There is however a continuing joint theological task for all Christians, of working out in thought, prayer and action the meaning and implications for all men of God's salvation, peace, love, justice. This involves the third world and any number of possible worlds. It requires the legacy of the European

Enlightenment as well as of African, Asian and American cultures, and it continues till the *eschaton*. What then of LT as a movement within a movement? As I understand the matter, it will always have a central role to play, as a particular dimension, one-sided if done in isolation from the rest of Christian theology as an exclusive concern. It is necessary as a constant reminder of the need for the concern of the gospel for the poor to remain at the heart of the Christian life. What do ye *more* than others?

I want to look now at one or two of the different emphases in LT, with a view to the development of LT as a universal dimension of theology. In Latin America the springs of LT lie in the presence of the right wing dictatorships. There is also an element of protest against racism. 'Latin America does have a continuous and consistent experience of "churches of the disinherited", but it has been too familiar to be recognized as such. It is the syncretism of Catholicism and Indian religious practices: a permanent social protest against cultural assimilation of the *Hispanidad* values of the white men who have run the public life of the continent since the Conquest.' (E. Norman, *Christianity in the Southern Hemisphere*, Oxford 1981, 56).

LT in Latin America has sometimes been Protestant, more usually Catholic. Though it is hard to generalize, we may think we can detect in the latter a somewhat more optimistic anthropology – things *can* be done, and in the former a greater sense of the radical ambiguity of all human striving, and a sharper distinction between the ultimate and the penultimate. In every area of doctrine we can see that LT is done not in a cultural or intellectual vacuum but in a particular context. In Leonardo Boff's christology, (*Jesus Christ Liberator*, London, 1980) we are concerned supremely not with a heavenly Christ who lives in and belongs to another realm, but with the Jesus of history who is involved in all the continuing conflicts of history. God's humanity in Jesus Christ is something which LT summons us to consider with new urgency.

In this stress on the achievability of God's kingdom *now*, LT especially in South America distinguishes itself from another form of LT, black theology, in North America. Black theology draws much of its strength from the social teaching of the Old Testament prophets, where LT stresses the New Testament. Black theology concentrates on the scandal of racism, where LT stresses economic exploitation, with closer links to Marxism. Naturally the growth of the literature has produced cross-fertilization, and so the critique of developmentalism, and the need for conscientization and contextualization have become part of a common currency from Latin America to South East Asia. (For the latter see Choan-Seng Song, *Third Eye Theology*, NY, 1979.) There have also, of course, been important European influences – I think of Gollwitzer, Hromadka, Lochman, Metz and Moltmann, and the 'worker priest' movement in France.

It is clearly possible to have theologies which need not necessarily use the title or even the style of LT, but which endorse its main emphasis. What sort of LT would be appropriate in this country? Without making party political points, it is clear that there is a very great deal that is not in harmony with the Christian specific commitment to people with the lowest levels of social advantage, in a society in which education, health and welfare services are falling apart, and where there are more than three million unemployed. Even full employment is not enough. It is pointless to produce employment merely by fuelling the armaments industry, by killing off the workers slowly by asbestosis, or whatever. Worse still is the habit, not unknown to British industry, of farming out dangerous or morally ambiguous industrial ventures to third world countries where standards are not enforced, where hunger may lead to the neglect of safety precautions or wider moral considerations, and where quick profits are to be taken. If we are to take seriously the central thrust of LT, then grave ambiguities at the heart of the entire fabric of our own industrialized society are exposed. To go back to some form of agrarian culture is only a romantic pipe-dream for the reasonably well-fed. Modern society is here to stay, together with the exploitation which appears endemic in East and West, North and South. It is in this sort of world that LT must form an important component of any theology, not to offer unqualified support for the prevailing plausibility criteria of culture, politics and society, but to challenge them with the searching and healing power of the Christian gospel.

Different approaches throw different sorts of light on the mystery of faith. We usually work out of a particular tradition, through our cultural background and (consequent) theoretical choices. We are likely to regard some traditions, properly understood, as more adequate to express the gospel than others. We can learn from all of them. LT is a theology of incarnation, and incarnation is at the heart of Christianity. (I am not here necessarily taking sides in our domestic incarnation and myth debate: there are thoroughly docetic incarnational theologies and deeply socially committed non-incarnational ones.) When the Word was made flesh and dwelt among us, God the creator committed himself without reservation to his created order, to risk, contingency and to solidarity through life, death and resurrection with the human race as it is, to bring it to what it shall be.

Incarnational theology can be anything but down to earth. LT can be anything but liberated. It can be as inhibited as any doctrinaire liberalism. However, the abuse does not take away the proper use, and so we must try to apprehend its central concern in a framework of theoretical charity. That is to say, we can neither take it over without thinking, nor pretend that we understand it and have always taken it into account. We have to bring it into our own critical reflection and action, prepared to argue and to learn.

We may reflect that, in so far as LT helps us to understand Jesus Christ as the sacrament of human salvation, it is up to us to support communities engaged in the theory and practice of LT in identification in prayer and worship and on every level. Of course, fascist communities have been sustained by the prayer and worship of the Churches. We believe that Christ is the ultimate truth. We must take the risk of believing that if we seek to be open to God and to each other, God will in fact use us as the instruments of his love, even if not always in the ways which we imagine.

Future shock
The question of how the future with its endless conflicting possibilities can be given due attention in the present becomes all the more pressing as the pace of social change accelerates. The vast problems of world hunger and of global confrontation make the responsible use of the present, that there may be a future in the first place for mankind, more urgent than most politicians care to admit. When Christian faith looks to the future, what does it see? One suggestion which I would make is that it sees the finite nature of human possibility, which at the same time has infinite possibility. Man is created not to realize the power of God in himself, but to achieve his own self-realization in the future as man – or, as I have stressed elsewhere, as woman. He seeks to be aware of his identity as a truly human person, with all that this may bring in its train. In faith this identity is already

given to him in Christ, in Christ he is a new creature. He does not have to find himself in action, but he already is. This is why he is free, free to act in love for others, in concrete responsibility for his fellow men. If he acts in order to become free he will probably bind himself and his neighbour in new chains. Already free in Christ, he is free to act in love, not as superman but as a man.

Here we might stop, on a note of 'happy ending' if the kingdom of God were already fully realized. But it is not. Man's position, before God, is not the same as his position before man. For millions the freedom to act in love is in practice often inhibited by crippling disability, political, social and physical. If we exist with thousands of our neighbours, at starvation level, with too few calories to allow normal physical or even mental development, then this condition is abhorrent to the love of God, and God himself suffers with those who suffer. I come back deliberately at the end of this study to the problem of world hunger. The resources to feed the hungry are there, the political will is lacking. Here is a case where politicians have singularly failed to provide adequate response. Indeed it is the political rivalries of East and West, of Marxist and non-Marxist of various sorts, which have served to exacerbate the problems of hunger in Africa, India and Asia.

Much has indeed been achieved through the Christian gospel to use human hands as the channel of God's love over the last two thousand years. To understate this achievement, and to underestimate the vast reservoirs of goodwill which through God's grace continue to inspire human beings to act throughout the world, people of various races, creeds and colours, would be a kind of ironic tribute to evil.[5] Much has been done and is being done. In all the areas of moral concern discussed in the previous pages there has been a tradition of gradual progress, with little scope for apocalyptic human transformation. Yet in the face of the ever-growing dimension of hunger and deprivation there can be no scope for ending on a note of satisfaction. We can only pray the ancient prayer for strength to become the instruments of God's love and his peace in his world. But that at least is cause for thanksgiving and for hope.

We cannot produce definitive solutions to the problems of Christian social ethics because the dimensions of the issues are constantly changing. This is, of course, all the more reason for having carefully considered guidelines as a basis for every fresh issue. Even as these pages are written the world political scene changes in important respects, challenging given assumptions. In Poland, in Afghanistan, in Zimbabwe and in numerous other spheres developments that could not be predicted in the recent past take place and call for new responses. In Uganda the removal from power of a monstrous tyrant has been followed, not by a return to peace and prosperity but by a new form of chaos, and renewed suffering and hunger. The well tried formulas of democratic succession do not always work. Are they then to be regarded as irrelevant in a new age? Most of us would want to affirm their continuing centrality. But even the best guidelines require intelligent and dedicated application to each particular changing situation. Only by remaining alert and combining flexibility with commitment to Jesus Christ can we hope to become the instruments of God's love for mankind in a swiftly changing world.

Notes

1. J. Moltmann, 'Towards a Political Hermeneutics of the Gospel,' In *New Theology*, 6,76.
2. Richard Shaull, 'Revolutionary Change in Theological Perspective,' in *Social Ethics*, ed. Gibson Winter (1968).

Originally for the WCC Conference on Church and Society, 1966.

3. See H.E. Tödt and T. Rendtorff, *Theologie der Revolution* (1968) and e.g. J. de Grouchy *The Church Struggle in South Africa* (1979) and Edna McDonagh, *The Demands of Simple Justice* (1980). See too J.B. Metz, *Theology of the World*, and *Towards Vatican III*, ed. Küng, Tracy and Metz; G. Gutierrez, *A Theology of Liberation* (1979) and *Puebla*, Report of the Second Conference of Latin American Bishops (1979).

4. E.R. Norman, *Christianity and the World Order* (1979). See the reply ed.

5. There is a history of Oxfam by Peter Gill, *Drops in the Ocean* (1970). See too J.V. Taylor, *Enough is Enough*, also the two Brandt Commission Reports, and the section on food and resources in *Faith, Science and the Future*, WCC, 1979. As the second Brandt Report sums up, 'The prospects for the future are alarming. Deteriorating economic conditions are likely to cause the disintegration of societies and create conditions of anarchy in many parts of the world.'

It may be reflected that the nuclear arms race has probably played a considerable part in precipitating world-wide recession. There have indeed been those who have argued that aid has done little or nothing to help the poorest people in aid-receiving countries, on the ground that governments committed to improving the material standards of the poor are rare in the third world. But this has been convincingly refuted by the responsible aid-giving bodies.

6. The following examples may serve as examples of a characteristic liberation perspective:

(a) 'A faith that does not become incarnate fades away. It disappears, and simply ceases to exist. Incarnation is the first law of revelation.' (J.L. Segundo, *The Community called Church* (1973), 37).

(b) 'The five biggest North American enterprises (General Motors, Ford, Standard Oil, General Electric and Chrysler) had in 1965 a turnover of about $55,255 million, almost seven times more than the total amount of the budgets for the same year of Brazil, the Argentine, Mexico, Chile,

Venezuela and Colombia which, together, scarcely totalled the sum of $8,177 million' (H. Camara, *Race against Time*, (1971), 91).

(c) 'The philosophy of oppression, perfected and refined through civilization as a true culture of injustice, does not achieve its greatest triumph when its propagandists knowingly inculcate it'. (J.P. Miranda, *Marx and the Bible* (1974), x1).

(d) 'An eschatological faith makes it possible for the Christian to invest his life historically in the building of a temporary and imperfect order with the certainty that neither he nor his effort is meaningless or lost.' (J.M. Bonino, *Revolutionary Theology comes of Age* (1975), 152).

(e) 'Whenever we feel the temptation to prudence, let us remember that "You have chosen the weak of the world in order to defeat the strong, and the stupid to confound the wise. For the prudence of the world is the enemy of God."' Louis Espinal, SJ, *Prudence*, quoted in *Doctrine and life*, February 1982, 115.

7. On poverty see especially R.H. Preston, *Church and Society*, especially ch.2, 'Christianity and economic man.'

Epilogue

God is the one whose essential nature is love. His creation takes place in, through and for love. This purpose is fulfilled in salvation through love, in Jesus Christ. Yet the conditions in which the great majority of the planet's population live are very far indeed from what most of us would regard as the kind of environment which is the fulfilment of the necessary conditions for loving concern. This challenge was met in the twentieth century by the churches in the development of the social gospel. The results remained discouraging: much was done, but there remained suspicion and only fragmentary realization of the aims. Theologians themselves complained that the gospel was about God not man. Others were suspicious of liberal complacency and superiority. In its place came the dialectical theologies and then the theologies of hope and revolution. Hopes were raised, often again to be cruelly disappointed, so raising yet more painful resentment. Few revolutions are so terrible in their aftermath as failed revolutions, while even successful ones often succeed only in turning one form of injustice into another. Once the rot has set in and civilized standards of equal justice have declined, the task of reconstruction is notoriously painful.

In my own view, the advocates of the social gospel were basically on the right lines. They may well have underestimated both the transcendence of God in their theological structure and the complexity of sociological structure and ideological conditioning in their practice.

They were not infallible, but in general they were willing to admit this, a virtue which their successors rarely possess. We cannot, however, solve the problem of Christian ethics in the 1980s with the solutions of the 1920s. It is one thing to say that we may not wish to espouse variants of Marxist theories of Christianity and other recent ideological alternatives on the right. It is quite another, and usually foolish, to fail to learn through examination and consideration of developing perspectives. As often, the key issue, which is so hard to perfect, is the ability to decide between the essential and the secondary in continuing debate about the theory and practice of ethics.

Inevitably Christians will take up different political views. Where there are no differences of opinion, something is usually wrong with political freedom. In socialist states in Eastern Europe there are and will be many Christians with political views which include Marxist elements in different ways – and others who reject such elements. In Western countries there will be those who adopt Conservative policies of the sort espoused by the right wing parties in Britain, France, Germany and America. In Africa and Asia there are variations of these stances and independent political positions arising from particular local situations. I myself am inclined to support a social democratic position on the centre-left of British politics.

Different positions involve tensions. It must be part of the Christian's task to try to ensure that such tensions are creative rather than destructive. There are actions and situations, in individual and in social ethics, which for the Christian of whatever political persuasion are always and everywhere just plain wrong, as we have indicated above. Where people are killed, where they are exploited and neglected, the call of God to discipleship is not served, in whatever name such exploitation may take place.

Only a minority of the world's population are Christians, and Christians are themselves far from immune to sin, to disobedience to God's will. Hence there arise those destructive tensions and rivalries which, in the greatest of modern disasters, prevent co-operation to feed the hungry, and in lesser but still often significant evils, encourage arms build-up, terrorization and subjugation of millions. Human rights and human dignity are not respected because of 'considerations of state', which preclude the allowing of freedom and dictate that a nation's gross national product be spent on defence.

It is useless to be naive and sentimental about these matters. National fears, racial fears and most of the other fears which diminish humanity are real fears and they have serious grounds. Yet the gospel insists that 'perfect love casts out fear' and that that love is present in, through and under human action by the grace of God. This is why realism need not be cynical realism. There is no need to underestimate the possibility of co-operation and mutual understanding among men. What is required is the patient and constant attempt to break down barriers, to develop differences into creative and constructive tensions rather than mutually self-destructive strife. For this process there is no instant solution. We must try to have more confidence in the means already given us in the gospel of God's love for man. This is the Christian contribution to ethics.

These are global issues, in the face of which the concerns of personal relationships and even of medical ethics may appear to pale into insignificance. Yet the Christian gospel invites faithfulness in small things as in great matters, in hidden decisions known only to God as well as in public engagement. No area of life is excluded from the reality, and the opportunity, of making Christian decisions.

Index of Proper Names

Index of Subjects